INVESTING
IN PATENTS

EVERYTHING STARTUP INVESTORS
NEED TO KNOW ABOUT PATENTS

RUSS KRAJEC

Investing in Patents

Everything Startup Investors Need to Know About Patents

ISBN: 0997410108
ISBN-13: 978-0997410105 (BlueIron Press)

This publication is designed to provide accurate and authoritative information in regard to the subject matter covered. It is sold with the understanding that the publisher is not engaged in rendering legal, accounting, or other professional service. If legal advice or other expert assistance is required, the services of a competent professional should be sought. *From a Declaration of Principles Jointly Adopted by a Committee of the American Bar Association and a Committee of Publishers and Associations.*

Limit of Liability/Disclaimer of Warranty: While the publisher and author have used their best efforts in preparing this book, they make no representations or warranties with respect to the accuracy or completeness of this contents of this book and specifically disclaim any implied warranties of merchantability or fitness of purposes. No warranty may be created or extended by sales representatives or written sales materials. The advice and strategies contained herein may not be suitable for your situation. You should consult with a professional where appropriate. Neither the publisher nor the author shall be liable for any loss of profit or any other commercial damages, including but not limited to special, incidental, consequential, or other damages.

BlueIron is a registered trademark of BlueIron, LLC. Any brand names and product names used in this book are trademarks, registered trademarks, or trade names of their respective holders.

The BlueIron business model is patent pending.

Published by BlueIron, LLC
Loveland, Colorado
www.blueironip.com/publishing

Acknowledgments

I would like to thank everyone who helped with the book: Bart Emery, Anne Blackburn, Seth Miller, Andy Blackstone, Charles and Andrew McGregor, David Cunningham, Matt Troyer, Bob Thilmont, Brian Murphy, Joe Mariconda, Joe Parker, Roger Ison, Joe Zell, Chris Sponheimer, Dean Becker, Gene Quinn, Renee Quinn, Jana Knapp, John Krajec, and Rachel Bader.

Contents

About This Book

There are many myths that are propagated amongst startup CEOs and their advisors about patents, and most startups—possibly 95% or more—have patents that are utterly worthless. The saddest thing is to hear startup CEOs trumpet how "protected" they are when they really have nothing.

This book presents a *new way of thinking about patents for startups*.

Patents, when viewed as an investment, have the same risks as startups: technology risk and market risk. When these risks exist, a patent has purely speculative value, and zero inherent value. As the risks are overcome, the patent begins to have actual, inherent business value. The best analogy is stock options, where the only real value comes when they are in-the-money.

Your author has experienced the invention and patent business from all sides: as an inventor with 30+ patents in multiple industries, as a patent agent/attorney who drafted nearly 1,000 patent applications for companies big and small, as an owner/broker of sizeable patent portfolios, as a co-founder and COO of an angel/venture backed startup that had nearly 100 patents, and as a CEO of BlueIron, an investment firm that invests solely in patents for startup companies.

BlueIron IP invests in patents. Our investment model is to pay all the patent costs for a startup, and let the startup finance those costs over the lifetime of the patent. Essentially, BlueIron allows the startup to take a mortgage on their asset so that the startup can deploy that capital elsewhere.

As a result of this business model, BlueIron must ensure that it holds *investment-grade* patents.[1]

The strategies and techniques in this book come from BlueIron's experience in making those investments.

---

[1] Appendix C discusses BlueIron's investment model in more detail, but that is not the focus of this book.

This book is not about the simple mechanics of the system, but how things *actually* work, with a special focus on startup companies. Startup companies have distinctly different needs—and different opportunities—than big companies, so their patent tactics and strategies should reflect that.

There are many unspoken and conflicted motivations of the parties in transactions relating to patents: from the initial attorney-client and attorney-inventor interactions, to the applicant-examiner interaction and the patent holder-infringement interaction.

One of the most helpful tools in our arsenal is BlueIron's due diligence checklist, which distills years of experience into a simple way of evaluating inventions prior to patenting, as well as evaluating existing patents during investment due diligence.

Far too many bootstrapped, angel, and venture-backed companies waste countless hours and dollars on worthless patents. This book is about recognizing how the system works and finding the best way to navigate the system to maximize your investment in the startup.

All readers are invited to visit http://investinginpatents.com/bonuses to receive several downloadable items that augment this book. These are free of charge to readers of this book.

My hope is that you learn something from this book and can apply it to your investments.

Russ Krajec

Book Summary

Key takeaway:

Patents, like businesses, only have value when the *business risk* is removed, not just the technology risk. Patents need to capture *business value*, not just cool technology.

Chapter 1: Making the Business Case for Patents.

Most patents—probably over 95%—are worthless. However, there is such a huge economic leverage that they still have value on a risk-adjusted basis. The return on investment depends on doing patents well.

From an investment viewpoint, patents have unique characteristics. Valuable ones capture the ***absolute best way of doing something*** AND are ***enforceable against an infringer***. From a practical standpoint, this means that the patents need to be detectable and need to be directed at the right actors.

There are serious tradeoffs when filing a patent application, and there are many circumstances where patents are ***damaging*** to a startup, not helpful.

The business purpose of a company's patent needs to track the ***business roadmap*** of the company, which is more important than the technology roadmap.

Common mistakes that startups make include: filing provisional applications (they waste the company's most precious resource: time), having inventors file their own patents, and not recognizing the cost of capital when spending on patents.

Exclusive licenses can be ***more valuable to a startup than owning their patents***. An exclusive license aligns incentives, but also eliminates unpredictable costs and makes better use of the company's high cost of capital. Operationally, exclusive licenses allow for more flexibility and can make the company immune from all sorts of lawsuits.

Chapter 2: How Startups Use Patents

Acquisition chances are always improved with good patent portfolios—not just from infringers but from the infringer's competitors, vendors, and customers. The enemy of my enemy is my friend.

Most startups think about patents as a moat around their investment in technology and marketing. Patents can be enforced in several ways ***without going to court and without being expensive.*** They can also give a startup access to competitor's technologies, help with open source software, and protect the classic razor/razor blade business.

The huge value of patents come when they ***multiply an investment.*** This comes from outbound licensing into other verticals, franchising solutions to others, spinning out technologies, negotiating with suppliers, and—the holy grail—when the patents are included in industry standards.

The secondary market for patents is much more sophisticated than people realize, and it is a great market for disposing of unused technology after a pivot.

Chapter 3: Managing the Process

Due diligence ***prior to patent filing*** is key to making sure time and money are not wasted on patents.

A startup needs to focus on patent quality because it does not have the budget to waste on lots and lots of patents, like big companies do.

CEOs and investors make bad decisions when they do not realize how narrow the patents might actually be. Be realistic about what can be protected, and avoid "wishful thinking" patents.

A roadmap for a startup's portfolio: ***The first patent is not going to be the most valuable patent, so do not treat it like it is.*** The valuable patents come when there is market validation and when problems are solved on the way to the vision.

Use ***market signals*** to determine when and what patents to file.

The attorney/client relationship <u>prevents</u> the attorney from giving advice, leaving the startup to fend for itself. The agency and fiduciary duties of the attorney infer huge liabilities on the attorney, and this extinguishes the attorney's ability to help. The attorney's first duty is to their own businesses, which is selling hours, not to the startup.

Chapter 4: Due Diligence on Startups

There are several places to look when evaluating a company's patents.

Assignments and provenance issues verify that the company actually has legal rights to the patents.

Inventorship issues are often overlooked, but they are one of the easiest ways to invalidate a patent. CEOs and company founders are notorious for making a mess of this. There are problems when there are too many inventors—and problems when there are too few.

Many inventorship issues happen in accelerators and incubators, which is why the ***secondary market applies a 50% discount to the value of any patent from a startup company that came from a startup accelerator***. A simple agreement by the accelerator would have prevented all the problems.

An invention rating checklist includes novelty, detectability, and actor analysis factors, as well as design-around analysis and alignment with internal and external business goals. This checklist can be used for inventions pre-filing, as well as during the patent process and for evaluating issued patents.

A simple rule-of-thumb for patent valuation is to calculate 25% of the gross margins of a product with the patented invention, then apply a discounted cash flow.

Appendix A: The invention ratings checklist.

Appendix B: A cost model for patent expenses.

Appendix C: An overview of the BlueIron investment model.

Introduction: The Patent System Is Broken—Or Is It?

The patent system is broken. How many times have we heard that?

This is a widely held belief that is relentlessly propagated, but as usual, there are two sides of the story.

The real problem has more to do with the <u>patent applicants</u> than the examiners and the legal system.

Part of our DNA as Americans is the story of the independent inventor toiling away in the garage. Our unwavering belief in the underdog is enshrined in the US Constitution:

The Congress shall have power… To promote the progress of science and useful arts, by securing for limited times to authors and inventors the exclusive right to their respective writings and discoveries…

This mandate in the Constitution is not going to go away, and the patent system will always be in place. It is our job to make the best of the system we have.

What is actually wrong with the system?

Several years ago, there were some big players who entered the patent system and began widespread enforcement on an industrial scale. And the patent community responded.

Because of the enormous cost of litigation, patent enforcement quickly took the form of patent extortion.[1] Any sane business person would pay the extortion, although they would grumble loudly and lobby Congress.

---

1   "Patent extortion" is when an enforcer holds up an alleged infringer for less than the price of a lawsuit. Whether the patent is valid or not never enters into the picture. Congress has since implemented the Inter Partes Reexamination (IPR) so that patents can be challenged without going to court (although IPR will still cost $200-500K). This does not "solve" the problem: it merely changes the economics of patent enforcement.

The patent extortion lawsuits had an interesting artifact:

Patent attorneys started to write horribly convoluted and twisted patent applications that nobody could understand. In fact, they brought it to a whole new level.

These types of patents were great fodder for Big Law, as one side of the firm would get paid tens of thousands to write the terrible patents, while the other side would get paid millions to enforce them.

This practice has spawned the widespread belief that patents should be written in some form of "legalese", and inventors often say that they cannot even figure out if their invention is in the patent application.

An entire generation of patent attorneys were trained under this style, and most still practice it. These attorneys generate patents that will be a scourge on the system for years to come.

The attorney/client relationship harms the patent process more than it helps.

The attorney/client and attorney/inventor relationships creates all kinds of strange, unintended side effects, most of which the client does not see or comprehend. One of the problems that clients never fully appreciate is the huge liability a patent attorney faces when giving *any type of business advice*—and that liability is amplified by the huge economic leverage of patents.

These problems put the attorney and client squarely **opposed** rather than aligned, and the client is left on their own for navigating the system.

The attorney's business is selling patents, and they often come across as respected, revered, or even feared by startup CEOs and inventors. Consequently, the attorney can easily hustle their client into filing the wrong patents at the wrong time with complete disregard to what is the business need of the client.

The client is left to fend for themselves, and often makes terrible business decisions because they do not have the experience or expertise.

This insidious process continues today, but…

There is a better way.

Patents should be understandable and easy to read.

It takes far more effort to write a clear, clean, direct, and comprehendible patent application than a giant, incomprehensible "pile of words".

- Understandable and readable patents get **better examination** from the USPTO, which means those patents are much more "legitimate" than those that are poorly written. Examiners find the best prior art, and feel confident allowing a case when they understand the invention.

- Understandable and readable patents get **better treatment** when used to negotiate in a business context, such as when negotiating with an infringer. When the patent is pushed across the table to an infringer, the infringer should read it, understand it, and say, "Oh no. I see how we infringe."

- Understandable and readable patents get **better results** when challenged, either in court or through the reexamination process, including Inter Partes Reexamination. Well written patents withstand reexamination, and the judges and juries—normal laypersons—render better decisions when they understand the patents.

Patents need to have real business value.

Patents should align with the business they are designed to protect. They need to capture the business's competitive advantage, period. When they don't accomplish this, the patents have no meaningful value.

Patents are a way of defending an investment in a company, as well as multiplying that investment. Patents can be used for keeping competitors at bay, managing supply chains, enforcing employment agreements, and even dictating how open source software can be used and distributed. Not only that, patents can be used to license technologies into other verticals, spin out new companies, offload older technologies, franchise businesses to other sectors or locations, or—the holy grail—get incorporated into an industry standard.

With a strong patent portfolio, a company is better positioned for long term success—as well as acquisition.

Patents have value only when the risks are removed.

Every business idea—and every patent—has two fundamental risks: a technology risk and a market risk. The technology risk is whether or not the idea will work, and the market or business risk is whether nor not someone will pay for the product or service.

Until the two risks are removed, a patent only has speculative value, much like an out-of-the-money stock option. The value only comes from the *possibility* that the product will work and someone will buy it.

When the product actually works and people pay for it, the product—and its patent—have real economic value.

It is easy to get patents on inventions that work. These fulfill the technology risk.

It is much more difficult to curate inventions that overcome both the technology and the market risks.

Many people look to their technology to find patentable ideas, but they are looking at only half of the risk and half of the equation.

The real value comes only when the business finds their customer's pain point and gives the customers solutions that they cannot live without.

For example, Apple famously has several patents[2] on a "slide-to-unlock" feature of its iPhone. These patents are not technically challenging to implement and are actually kind of gimmicky. However, the slide-to-unlock feature addresses a very strong customer pain point: how to unlock a phone that does not have any buttons?

The business or market value of this feature is tremendous, much more than many of the "technical" features of the iPhone. These patents were so valuable from a business standpoint that they were

---

2   US 8,286,103, US 8,046,721, and US 7,657,849. These patents were litigated in the ongoing *Apple v Samsung* patent lawsuits.

asserted against Samsung. Of all the hundreds or possibly thousands of patents that Apple could have enforced against Samsung, Apple chose the slide-to-unlock patents. This is probably the highest validation of patents that address a *customer value* as opposed to a highly technical advancement.

How to get an investment-grade patent.

Investment grade patents are curated in two steps. The first is saying "No" to many inventions. Far too many patents are written for the wrong reasons. An invention may be "cool" and exciting, but if it does not directly relate to products produced by the company, it is not worth pursuing.

The second step is designing the patent application to have direct commercial value. This is about capturing the **customer value** of the invention in the patent, and doing so in the context of the business landscape. It also takes constant vigilance throughout the patent process to nurture the application so that it aligns with the business.

1   Making The Business Case For A Patent

Patents are business assets first and foremost. If the patent fails to add substantial business value, there is no reason to have it.[1]

An angel or venture capital investor typically requires a 10x return on investment in 5 years. This amounts to a 56% year over year increase in company value. The assumption is that a startup CEO will invest capital to achieve this astronomical growth. Ideally, each expenditure should yield 56% per year growth or higher.

Consequently, an investor would like the money invested in a patent needs to produce that same level of return or higher.

The business value of a patent is not easily calculated. Sometimes, the mere presence of a patent can deter a competitor from entering a market, the value of which is impossible to quantify. The business value might be easier to quantify when a startup is able to negotiate with a supplier to trade some exclusive rights to the patent in exchange for an investment in capital by the supplier.

Some people view patents as merely an insurance policy that protects an investment from being copied by competitors. Some investors do not like insurance policies because in some ways they dilute the high risk exposure that they seek. These investors have a "burn the ships" mentality. Other investors see patents as mitigating excessive risks.

But patents offer much more than reducing risk.

Patents can have extraordinary value in multiplying an investment. This occurs when the company can stake out a broad landscape for itself and keep competitors at bay, when technology can be

---

[1]   For the sake of completeness, there are some business reasons for getting even a terrible patent. These include putting "patent pending" or "patented" on products, and for appeasing unsophisticated investors. These types of patents are very short-sighted and not "investment-grade" because they fail to generate value at the same rate or in the same way as an investment in a business needs to generate value.

licensed to competitors and non-competitors, when inventions are spun out into new companies focused on a new vertical market or licensed into industry standards, or many other scenarios, including extracting technology from a competitor.

Well-designed patents can have a dramatic multiplying effect on the remaining investment in a company.

Good patents have enormous economic leverage. Consider that the cost to acquire a US patent averages $50,000 to $60,000, but the best of those assets can produce license fees (or verdicts in a lawsuit) of $500,000,000 or more over their lifetime. The secondary patent market is a good indicator: the average patent can sell for $200,000 to $500,000[2] or in the neighborhood of 3-10x their original cost.

However, most patents are worthless because they are researched poorly, badly written, not managed correctly, or suffer from a host of other problems. Most importantly, <u>most patents are worthless because they are not aligned with a business purpose.</u>

The underlying theme of this book: **patents are only valuable when they match real business needs of a real company.**

1.1 Startup Company Valuation Goes Up With Patents

High quality, investment-grade patents can have spectacular impact on a startup's valuation. In the early stages of a company, especially when technology risks and market risks abound, the patents may be the most valuable asset the company has.

An investment in a single, well-crafted, defensible patent that matches a company's business prospects can easily raise the value of the company by the cost of the patent multiplied 10x—if not more.

---

2   The average price for a patent on the secondary market varies wildly from quarter to quarter and from year to year. This is due in part from the lack of data, since the data are based on publically available transactions, as well as the sparseness of the data, since in any quarter, there may be only a small handful of transactions. However, the range of $200-500K/patent has held up over the last decade.

It should be noted that these prices reflect the risk-adjusted *enforcement value* of the assets, not the total value of royalties that could be captured by infringement, which would be much higher.

There are several methods for valuing patents, many of which mimic the valuation methods for businesses as a whole.[3]

One simple way of calculating a patent's value is a reasonable royalty rate method based on the 25% rule. Determine the total addressable market of the invention and the product's margins. The patent value is approximately 25% of gross margins times the total addressable market.[4]

Note that this is one of the more conservative ways to value a patent. A startup that had 100% of a market that was completely protected by a patent would receive 100% of the gross margins.

Remember that patents have a lifespan of nearly 20 years[5], so the value of the patent should reflect royalties on a discounted cash flow basis over the 20 years. Reduce the total value by various risk factors, and that produces a value of the patent.

For startup companies who have not proven the technology or who do not have market traction, the value of the patent (and the value of the company) assumes that the company will be successful, but on a risk-adjusted basis.

Any valuation of a startup company should include a valuation of the patent assets as well. In many cases, the patent assets may be the most valuable assets the company has.

Over time and in highly competitive marketplaces, a startup company with a well-positioned patent may attract competitors, and those competitors may infringe the startup's patents. In this case, the value of the patents are based on the actual royalties that could be collected from the infringers.

3   In the due diligence section later in Chapter 4, the 25% rule-of-thumb valuation analysis is discussed in more detail. There are dozens of more complicated ways to calculate an invention's value.

4   Note that *sometimes* the 25% rule only applies to the improvement in a product, not to 25% of the gross margins of the entire product. A license on a cell phone antenna will not necessarily be applied to 25% of the entire phone.

5   The patent expires 20 years after the date of filing, but the Patent Office will extend the patent term to be a minimum of 17 years. The Patent Term Extension occurs when the Patent Office takes longer than 3 years to examine the patent. Like with everything from the USPTO, there are exceptions and rules, so the details of a specific case may differ.

1.2 The Ugly Truth—Most Patents are Worthless

Most patents are worthless, and for startup companies, this author's estimate is that at least 95% are worthless.[6]

A survey of several large patent holders revealed that they believe that less than 10% of their portfolio has high or medium-high value.[7] Remember that these are professionally managed patent portfolios from companies with lots of resources. How much worse will the startups be, when they do not have the focus, expertise, experience, or management tools to professionally curate and manage their patents?

Patents become worthless for many reasons, most of which can be avoided, and some of which cannot.

As with stock options, there is a possibility that the market may not come to the invention and that the initial guess was wrong. To some extent, this can be avoided through better due diligence in the marketplace, but in reality, this is part of the overall risk of any enterprise.

When the startup company is successful, it forces the market to come to the invention. This is when a patent has value.

Most patents are worthless for reasons that can be avoided. Techniques for avoiding worthless patents are found throughout this book, and many of them are discussed on Chapter 4 on Due Diligence.

The biggest factor, however, is alignment between the patent and the business. When the patent properly captures the core elements of a (successful) business, the patent has real value, provided none of the other common mistakes are made in the process.

---

6   It should not be lost on the angel investor that the patent "failure" rate is roughly equivalent to the overall failure rate of startup businesses.

7   See Figure 2 of "Patent Portfolios: Quality, Creation, and Cost" by Larry M. Goldstein on page 110. From the figure, the companies surveyed valued 0.9% of their portfolio "High" and another 7.3% as "Medium High".

1.3 Characteristics of Patents for Designing Good Business Assets

Notwithstanding the fact that most patents are worthless, the ones that are worth something are typically worth a huge fortune.

Patents have incredible economic leverage. How else can a solo inventor in a garage create something, enshrine it in a patent, and receive hundreds of millions of dollars? This only happens because of the patent.

In this section, we explore some of the nuances and interesting characteristics of patents from a business perspective.

1.3.1 Patents Have Big Value Only When They are Infringed

Patents are infringed when someone uses the technology, either intentionally or unintentionally.[8] Either way, the infringer is using protected technology.

The implications are that if a competitor could design around the patent, there is no real value to the patent.

Another way to state the same thing is:

Patents only have value when they protect the <u>very best</u> way to do something.

If there are better alternatives, the patent is worthless.[9]

Every imaginable alternative to an invention needs to be considered in due diligence. This forms the basis of an economic value of the invention.

With the baseline of a best design-around alternative, we can then compare the invention to the best alternatives and start putting a rough dollar value on the invention.

The $3 improvement to the $10 product.

---

8   Like an in-the-money call option, the big value for a patent comes only when it is infringed. Out-of-the-money call options, like non-infringed patents, only have *potential* or *speculative* value.

9   If there are functionally equivalent alternatives, the competitive value of the patent is only the engineering cost to design and implement the alternative.

The economic analysis is easy to do on the back of an envelope. Take the economic advantage of the invention over the best alternative and multiply it by the total addressable market. If an invention has a $0.10 advantage over the alternatives and there are 10,000,000 units sold per year, the economic advantage is $1,000,000/year.

The economic advantage can be directly measurable, such as cost reduction of a manufactured product. Sometimes, the economic advantage is not easily measurable, such as the additional money that a consumer might pay to have an inventive feature to a software product.

When the economic advantage is not easily measurable, it may be helpful to run some A/B or split tests with a group of consumers to determine any additional money that a consumer might pay for the inventive feature.

Entrepreneurs and inventors almost always have an inflated view of what their inventions are worth. The true worth comes out when the market dictates the value, which can come when the product is in the market, or when patents are being sold on the secondary market. The market is always a much more realistic view of the value than an inventor's.

1.3.2 Patents Only Have Value When They Can Be Enforced

It is far easier than one might think to create patents that are unenforceable. The dynamics of the attorney/inventor/client relationship, as discussed in Chapter 3, cause a lot of weirdness, and the result is that the patent attorney does not have much incentive to make sure the patent is enforceable. This is an unintended side effect of our legal system, but something every CEO and inventor needs to know.

Patent enforcement is a very complex subject, with lots and lots of case law, rules, exceptions to those rules, and other issues. There are plenty of corner cases where awful patents were successfully enforced, and where excellent patents were not enforceable. But there are some simple and easy-to-understand rules, most of which will seem obvious, but are not put into practice:

Patents need to be detectable.

This may appear to be an obvious statement, but people pour money into patents where infringement simply cannot be detected.

When looking at an invention (or an issued patent), one of the first questions should be: "Can I detect that my competitor is using this invention?"

If there is no way to tell that a competitor is performing the same method or manufacturing the same product, how could that patent ever be enforced? The answer: it cannot be enforced and is therefore worthless.

Most software patents are awful and not just because they protect software.[10] Most software patents are awful because the patent owner could never detect that a competitor uses their invention. Consider a gloriously complex and innovative artificial intelligence method for analyzing a bunch of data and returning a result. The algorithm runs deep inside a competitor's datacenter, where we will never have access.

Could we ever tell that the competitor is using the exact same algorithm as in our patent? No. That patent is worthless and the invention would have better been kept as a trade secret.[11]

In another example, Tropicana famously has a patent on fresh-squeezed orange juice.[12] The patent is a detailed analysis of how to blend different varieties of oranges throughout the season to achieve a consistent product. This is because each variety has a different color factor and sugar content, and those factors further

---

10   Software patents get a bad rap because many people, including startup CEOs, make bold statements about how broad their patent owners and alleged infringers read the patents and think they are incredibly broad and all-encompassing, when in truth, they tend to be unbelievably narrow. This comes out in sabre rattling between companies, as well as the typical grandiose statements CEOs make to investors—the best ones are those that capture the most elegant solution to a problem. These look "obvious" in hindsight, but are often the result of an incredible amount of hard work.

11   There are tricks for dealing with this situation, such as writing a patent around the detectable effects of the algorithm, or focusing on the interfaces within a software product (an API, user experience, administrative user interface, etc.)

12   US Patent 6,143,347 "Early Season Not From Concentrate Orange Juice and Process of Making."

change depending on when they are harvested. Tropicana's patent reflects a lot of work went into this research.

However, Tropicana's claim 46 requires "at least about 1 percent by weight of a stored orange juice." Could Tropicana take a sample of a competitor's orange juice and tell that it had "stored orange juice"? No. That claim is impossible to detect, therefore unenforceable and commercially worthless. [13]

Patents must be directed at the right actor.

A key to enforcement is making sure the patent captures the actions of the actor we want to stop. It goes without saying that the business value of a patent comes from enforcing the patent against someone. Who is the actual infringer?

A simple example may be a company that has heat-moldable inserts for a ski boot. A consumer may heat up the insert in boiling water, then mold the insert to their foot, then place the insert in the ski boot.

If the patent claims describe these steps, who is the infringer? The steps are something done by the consumer—the company's customer. Can the company sue their customers? No. The patent is worthless.

In a more complicated example, there was a company that made wireless components for the cable television industry. These were wireless transmitters that were mounted on a utility pole or pedestal outside the consumer's home and made a wireless "last-mile" connection to the consumer. The invention removed the need for a coaxial cable to be run to the subscriber's house. [14]

The company's customers were MSOs (cable system operators). The company's competitors were other equipment manufacturers who sold hardware to the cable operators.

The company's patent claims required a box that was mounted outside the home and broadcasted wirelessly into the home.

---

13   There are problems with all of the other independent claims as well, rendering the *entire patent* unenforceable.

14   The invention was actually conceived as a noise-reduction mechanism when the cable systems were just beginning to provide two-way communications years ago. By eliminating the physical connection to the cable plant, electronic noise inside the consumer's house would not propagate upstream and cause problems.

Who was the infringer of the patent?

It turns out that the actual infringer was the cable network operator, not the company's competitors. The network operator was the one that mounted the box, provided the receiver inside the home, and caused the various signals to be transmitted.

The patent could not be enforced against their competitors, only their customers.

Could the company sue their customer? Not without alienating them from doing business. In that context, the patent is worthless.[15]

The result was that the company ultimately had an enforceable patent, but one that could only be used to sue their own customers. After the company folded, the patent was transferred to another company who eventually enforced the patent against the cable network operators.

How did this happen?

With this invention, the original claims were for a device that had the radios and signal processing equipment. If those claims were allowed, the patent would have been directly enforceable against a competitor and would have been exactly what the startup wanted. However, to get around a rejection by the patent examiner, the patent attorney amended the claims so that the invention had to be mounted on a utility pole and broadcast into a user's home.

It was not until the amendment that the claims went from being directed at a direct competitor to being directed at a consumer. The amendment only added a few short lines of text to the claims, and the company was ecstatic that they had a very valuable patent.

This is a great example of how the focus of a patent can change dramatically by some otherwise innocuous work by a patent attorney. In this case, a great patent that could have protected an

---

15   This situation might have a case for contributory infringement, inducement to infringe, indirect infringement, or some other non-direct theory of infringement. In each of those cases, the infringement is much more difficult to establish, and there is a lot of problems in enforcement. At the inventing phase, there are several tricks for addressing this problem, such as reforming the invention to describe the product produced by a competitor.

entire company turns into a boat anchor that they could never actually use.[16]

This story illustrates why the enforcement analyses need to be done at each stage of the patent process. First, the detectability and enforcement factors help determine whether or not to get a patent on a specific invention. As negotiations happen with the patent examiner, these factors should be applied to each claim and each amendment to the claim. Lastly, the enforcement factors help determine whether an issued patent has value.

1.3.3 Patents are Twenty Year Assets

The lifespan of a patent is 20 years from the filing date. This is a very long time, especially given the life expectancy of a startup company.

The patent is essentially a bet that the market will "come to the invention" over the next 20 years.

Ideally, a startup company will force the market to come to the invention through their marketing and eventual sales of a product. However, the patent is a bet that the market may come to the invention by its own natural and unpredictable powers.

A patent's twenty year lifespan means that the thought process for building a valuable patent differs from a typical startup's time horizon. Someone concerned with the patent value will be focused on the sweet spot between 5 and 15 years away, when patents typically sell for the highest amount.

The startup, on the other hand, is concerned about an 18 to 24 month window to reach their milestones.

The tension between the patent viewpoint and the startup viewpoint can be helpful to the startup. The typical startup CEO is focused on the issues at hand—raising money, rolling out a minimum viable product, and landing sales, but the CEO devotes very little time to long term forecasting. The patent portfolio is a great mechanism

---

16   The patent in this example eventually made its way to the secondary patent market nearly a decade after the company imploded, returning at least some value to the shareholders.

to force some analysis of the long-term value of the company and its technology.

1.3.4 Good Patents are Written from the Claims

Unless someone has been involved in patent litigation or has some other unfortunate experience with patents, most people do not understand patent claims.

The claims are at the end of the patent and are the strict, legal definition of the invention. They are often tersely written and can be hard to understand, but they are the actual invention. Everything else in the patent is either supporting the claims or purely fluff.

A good patent starts with the claims.

A well written patent starts with the legal definition of the specific invention, then supports the patent claims with a description of how to make or use the invention.

Many people, especially inventors who write their own patents, describe a product, but the product is not an invention. A product is *one* way the invention can be embodied, but is not the *only* way.

For example, a product might be a heat-moldable insert that a consumer adjusts to their foot, then places in their shoe. However, the invention is making an orthotic easy enough to make that it could be marketed directly to consumers. The invention could also be the business concept of making an otherwise professionally-fitted product into something that a consumer could do.

When the invention is crafted in the form of the business value to the consumer, the patent description takes a much different form than a description of a heat-moldable insert.

The claims are important because the patent can only be enforced when someone infringes each and every element of the claim. Most inventors and CEOs think that their product is 'protected' by a patent because the rambling description is so broad, but the actual item that is protected may be the extremely narrow elements that the examiner actually approves.

1.4 The Tradeoffs and Considerations for Patents

Patents are not free. There is the economic cost, but there are business costs as well. The business costs include opportunity costs, time and energy commitments, and the like, but the biggest business cost is the quid pro quo with the government.

There are times when a patent becomes a substantial negative liability, not just because of the cost, but because of the requirements to publically disclose the company's trade secrets in exchange for the limited right of a patent.

1.4.1 Patent Costs

The average patent in the US costs $56,525.00. This is based on the American Intellectual Property Lawyers Association's bi-annual survey. Appendix B lays out the costs in detail.

The costs come in tranches. After a meaningful search ($4000), writing the patent application ($12,000), and US filing fees ($800), the initial outlay is $16,800. There is an additional $4,000 if a PCT or international application is filed, another $4000 for a total of $20,800.

The patent examination process costs, on average, $24,175 and can stretch over 3 to 7 years. These costs dribble out at $4,000 intervals as rejections come from the examiner and the attorney writes responses. This cost includes probabilities for going up on appeal as well. This is the most variable part of the patent costs, as most of the other costs are relatively fixed.

The issue fees are $1,800 when the patent is granted, and there are maintenance fees paid at 3.5, 7.5, and 11.5 years. This brings the grand total to $56,525.

Note that this is the US average. Some patents will cost less, and some substantially more.

Most patents can take 3 to 7 years before they are allowed by the examiner.

However, programs such as the PCT-Patent Prosecution Highway[17] can accelerate the process and the patent will often issue within 12 months. Note that this will compress the schedule so that the prosecution costs of $24,175 will be spent in 12 short months.

1.4.2 Cost Drivers for Patents

There are several factors that cause the patent costs to vary.

The most expensive (and variable) cost is getting through the patent examination process. There are cases that sail through and get allowed on the first look, but there are also cases that seem to take forever. Every attorney has some cases that are pending for 10+ years.

Almost always, patent costs can be reduced by good due diligence. Obviously, a patent search will avoid submitting a patent application for something that has already been disclosed.[18]

The costs are also reduced by good drafting. A clearly written, easy to understand patent application is much easier for the examiner to review. The examiners tend to do a much better job when they search, so that they can focus on the point of novelty and get the case allowed.

These are the cost drivers for getting the patent through the examination process, but *a patent's cost does not reflect the commercial value.*

1.4.3 Big, Expensive Firms Tend to do a Worse Job on a Startup's Patents than Small Firms

Many people use price as a substitute metric for quality.

Startup CEOs, especially ones that had experience in large corporations, can get addicted to the status symbol of Big Law.

---

17   The USPTO has two other programs for expediting the patent in the US. One of the programs is called Track One, which costs about the same as PCT-PPH, but has several restrictions. The other method is Accelerated Examination, and that program is so encumbered with problems that it is virtually malpractice to use it.

18   One caveat of patent searches is to remember that patent applications are published 18 months after filing. Any patent search will miss any patent applications filed in the last year and a half. This is an inherent risk of all patent applications.

These CEOs are easy to spot because they will tell everyone who their attorneys are.

The way the sausage gets made in Big Law is hideous. Big Law needs Big Clients to pay the bills, and consequently Big Clients get all of the attention. A startup CEO may meet with a Big Law partner, but rest assured that the work is being done by an inexperienced first year associate in a windowless back room.

The pure economics of the situation is that startups are a waste of Big Law resources, and startups will never get the attention they deserve, no matter how friendly the partner is. There is just no incentive for Big Law to waste their opportunity costs on small startups.[19]

The matter becomes even worse when Big Law does work at cut rate prices. The pyramid scheme of law firm partnerships only work when they can bill full rate. Cut rate work by Big Law only ensures that the *quality* is also cut rate.[20]

Small firms do not have the Big Clients, so they have more attention to devote to helping a startup company.

There is a big difference between just doing a job and doing a job well. When writing an investment-grade patent, the patent attorney needs to absorb, digest, and describe all of the technical and business aspects of an invention. This takes enormous amount of brain power to do well. It cannot be done effectively when hurried or rushed—or when there are more important clients to serve.

An investor should not be impressed by a startup company that has legal work done by the most expensive lawyers available. The work product should be questioned because the incentive to do

---

19   Another factor with Big Law is that they can get into a conflict between a startup and a Big Client. This represents a huge opportunity cost, because Big Law would not be able to pursue a Big Client that competes with a startup.

Big Law often gets in trouble for trying to represent two competing companies. See http://patentlyo.com/hricik/2016/03/million-verdict-conflict.html and *Axcess International, Inc. v. Baker Botts LLP* (Tex. App. Dallas March 2016).

20   From a liability standpoint, the risk exposure for shoddy lawyering is minimal because the startup is unlikely to survive past two or three years.

good work has vanished, and the judgment of the CEO should be also questioned.[21]

1.4.4 The Quid Pro Quo

New inventors are often unaware of the *quid pro quo* that is fundamental to the patent system.

The inventors must show the world their innermost secrets of how to make or use their invention. In exchange, the government grants a limited right in the form of a patent.

One of the options for the inventor is to *not* to file a patent, but simply to keep their invention secret. The most common examples are the formula for Coca Cola or Colonel Sander's secret herbs and spices. Both of these examples could have been patented, but were not. From a business standpoint, these were the right decisions.

There are many examples of patents that had virtually no value because the claims were undetectable, unenforceable, or ridiculously narrow. In the process of getting a worthless patent, the company gave up their complete roadmap for how to manufacture and use their product.

These patents are not just a waste of money, but their competitive advantage is eviscerated by disclosing everything they know. The bottom line:

Some patent applications can be very damaging to a startup company.

Part of the analysis prior to filing a patent is to first estimate how broad or narrow the patent might be, then evaluate whether the patent—at that breadth—would be worth pursuing. This analysis starts with a patent search.[22]

Many investors want to check the box of "is it patented?". However, most investors are not aware that the patent will post all the company

---

21   There are always exceptions to the rule. For example, very complex securities or regulatory issues might be worth hiring very experienced, but narrowly focused attorneys. For day to day legal issues, however, Big Law typically provides a worse work product than smaller firms when Big Law is working at a discount.

22   Chapter 4 includes a short tutorial for how to do classification-based patent searches.

secrets online for all competitors—with virtually no benefit to the company. The decision to get a patent or not needs to be made carefully and thoughtfully, and many companies are better off with no patent protection.

How does this happen?

One very typical scenario is when a startup company thinks they need to get a patent and do so in a panic, often just before they do a presentation for the first time and publically disclose their invention to the world.

It is conventional—but a terrible practice—for patent attorneys to file provisional patent applications in this situation.[23] The attorneys get called at the last minute and grab whatever information is available, slap a cover sheet on it, and file a provisional patent application.

Some companies put their pitch decks, pages of lab notebooks, internal decision making processes, internal financial projections, even source code for their software in the provisional patent application. This is done with the mistaken belief that the provisional application will not be made public.[24]

This situation happens because the patent attorney figures they will sort it out later. Maybe something in one of the documents will support some patent claims that we want to file a year from now.

From the patent attorney's perspective, the larger pile of information, however disorganized, the more likely it will be that they can find something patentable.[25]

---

23 The US allows for a "provisional" patent application, which serves as a placeholder for a "non-provisional" patent application, which must be filed within a year after the provisional patent application. The non-provisional application is the only type of patent application that gets examined by the USPTO.

Provisional patent applications are often touted as the "poor man's patent". As described later, provisional patent applications are one of the big mistakes that startup companies make with their patents.

24 When the subsequent non-provisional application is published, the provisional application then becomes part of the public record. If there is no subsequent non-provisional application, the provisional application will remain secret forever. But if it was abandoned, it was a waste of time.

25 This is just another example of how the attorney's interest in getting patents can severely compromise the company's interests.

From the client's perspective, they have given up their most valuable trade secrets, including all their internal documents, in exchange for their patent.[26]

As will be explained below in Chapter 3, the first patent that a company does is often the <u>least valuable</u> patent. This makes sense because both the technology and business risks are the highest at this stage. Why give up the most to get the least?

What to do if this happens?

How should an investor respond when a startup files these types of "kitchen sink" provisional patent applications?

One option to consider is to abandon the provisional patent application and start all over.

This appears to be a very drastic measure on the surface, but not as drastic as it sounds. In many cases, these types of patent applications are very thin when it comes to describing the actual patent claims.

Consequently, this provisional application does not actually give the right of priority to the filing date, so the real right of priority would only start with the second, non-provisional application.

In this case, the company did not have decent protection to begin with, so abandoning the provisional application and writing a good non-provisional application has no downside. In fact, there is a big upside because the company's trade secrets are not published.

1.4.5 Patents Must be Filed Early and Cannot be Changed

Another similarity to a stock option is that for a patent, the entire bet must be placed today, and it cannot be changed over the 20 year life of the patent.

While the US grants a one-year grace period to file a patent after a public disclosure or offer for sale, in Europe and most of the world

---

26   The company would have a very hard time enforcing any of their "trade secrets" when they publically disclose them in a patent application, because they would no longer be trade secrets. For example, a disgruntled employee may join a competitor and bring all the trade secrets with them, and the company could not bring a claim against the employee to try to stop them from sharing the "trade secrets".

the disclosure rules require that a patent must be filed before any public disclosure, with no grace period. [27]

These requirements paint the patent applicant in a corner. The patent must contain all the information the inventor knows about the invention, but there is rarely any market data to see if the invention actually makes business sense.

This combination heightens the risk factors of a patent. If the initial assumptions about the viability of the invention are wrong, the patent is likely to have little or no value. The assumptions are two-fold: the technology assumption that the invention operates as intended, and the market assumption that people will buy it.

The technological risk can be mitigated by prototyping and testing, but the market risk is much more difficult given the disclosure restrictions.

There are ways to do limited market testing under Non-Disclosure Agreements, but these are not nearly as effective as a large scale marketing and sales effort, which will reveal the true value of the patent.

1.4.6 Risk Analysis

Like every business decision, the decision to file or not file a patent application hinges on whether the benefits will outweigh the costs on a risk-adjusted basis.

There were plenty of risks mentioned above, but a patent's enormous economic leverage can outweigh the risks.

Many of the risks can be mitigated by due diligence prior to filing a patent.

Small companies do not have the budget to pursue hundreds or thousands of patents, so the best strategy is to curate individual patents to meet specific business needs. This will minimize waste in the portfolio and maximize value for each asset.

There is a cost to doing due diligence. Patent searches, competitive analyses, working on design around alternatives, and other due

---

27   Many investors will refuse to sign Non-Disclosure Agreements, which could cause a company to disclose their invention. Their own portfolio companies could lose international patent rights in some cases for such a policy.

diligence items take time and effort, but the difference between an investment-grade patent and a worthless patent is just a little extra effort.

1.5 A Business Purpose for the Portfolio

Most large technology companies have professionally-managed patent portfolios. They typically manage a portfolio in-house, because their patent portfolio is a core competency at some level.

The integrated circuit industry, for example, has evolved to the point where they are essentially patent licensing entities. They no longer have fabrication facilities, and they only create designs and license them for manufacture.

IBM is well known for generating billions of dollars a year licensing and selling patents. Microsoft makes more money licensing their extensive portfolio of mobile phone patents to Android phone manufacturers than it makes selling its own mobile phones.

All of these companies generate significant revenue from their patent portfolios and have an in-house team who manages their portfolios.

The key difference between professionally-managed portfolios and patents that are done by startups is that there is method and purpose to the process.

A startup CEO typically outsources the patent portfolios to patent attorneys, and the CEOs do not actively manage the portfolio.[28] As discussed in Chapter 3, there is a fundamental disconnect between the patent attorney and the business interests of the clients, resulting in the lack of oversight and management by the company.

Every dollar spent by a startup company has to be spent for a business purpose, and the patent portfolio is no exception.

In the broadest sense, the business purpose of a patent portfolio is to put the company in the best position to succeed. Success may be keeping other competitors outside of the company's market which protect a company's high margins. Success may be to license

---

28 Sometimes, startup CEOs will feel forced into micromanaging the patent attorneys. This is always a disaster, causing passive-aggressive behavior on the part of the attorney and putting a huge burden on the CEO to get involved in even the most mundane issues.

technologies to other vertical markets through a spin out company. Success may be to cross license technologies with a supplier to get a competitive advantage in pricing or market exclusivity.

Startup companies have a portfolio that begins with one patent and grows from there. One easy mistake to make is to try to do it all with one patent. The first patent is the riskiest, but subsequent patents will have less risk as the technology and market risks are reduced.

A good portfolio will develop on a thoughtful, deliberate roadmap that has two main pathways: a technology roadmap and a business roadmap.

The technology roadmap will foresee where technology may develop, then place patent "bets" along the way. The business roadmap may attempt to see where consumer needs and wants will develop, and place patent "bets."

1.5.1 Technology Roadmap

The technology evolution may be much easier to see and forecast than the business roadmap, but the business roadmap is much more valuable—if the bet is right.

Most companies build their patent portfolio by protecting their current and future products. Often, these patents may be influenced by expected developments in the technology landscape.

Good portfolios go further.

A good patent portfolio tries to anticipate technology developed by the company, but also complimentary technology developed by other companies. A good portfolio anticipates how new technology will interact or change the company's products.

A portfolio built on the roadmap of how products and technology will develop will be very valuable and open up many business opportunities. But there is much more to a good portfolio.

1.5.2 The Business Roadmap

The business roadmap is much more difficult to factor into the patent portfolio, but is where the value is. The portfolio typically starts by focusing on a defensible moat to keep competitors from directly competing, but then expands to many other purposes.

As the business grows, some of the business weaknesses may be protected by building a patent portfolio to shore up those weaknesses. For example, a supplier or competitor may have superior technology in some aspect. A patent portfolio may include patents directly aimed at cross licensing to trade for that technology.

Many large companies will have internal portfolios directed at specific competitors. These patents might be narrow, but they are very likely to be patents that are infringed by specific competitors by specific products.

This gives the company freedom to operate in the space.

Even though the big company may infringe patents of their smaller and more nimble competitors, the big company may have several patents that the smaller company infringes. Most of the time, these patents are never litigated, but they stand as a mutually assured destruction countermeasure if the smaller competitor were ever to assert their patents. This turns into a "silent cross-license" to a competitor's portfolio.

The business's strengths may be emphasized by the patent portfolio. When a customer-centric insight occurs, the most valuable patents will be those that cover the solution to the newly-discovered customer need.

A strong technology and business presence in a specific area may be bolstered and improved with additional sets of patents. This will allow the company to have a domineering presence when setting industry standards or negotiating from a position of power.

1.5.3 Startup Companies Often Fall Way Behind in Patents

Startup companies are focused on the present: making the next milestone, showing market traction before the next investment round, and getting the minimum viable product into the market. Patents, on the other hand, are assets that might be available in 12 months, but most likely are positioning the company for value in

3-5 years down the road, and maybe even 10-15 years down the road when other companies are infringing.

Portfolio strategies for startup companies tend to develop in a reactionary basis, not a proactive basis. A company gets sued by a competitor, and the company figures out that it needs patents to negotiate. Building a portfolio from a defensive standpoint can be very expensive. Facebook had virtually no patents in 2012, then famously purchased a large number of patents from AOL in a billion dollar transaction.[29] Many startup companies experiencing incredible growth spurts wind up buying portfolios or paying steep license fees when they have nothing to trade.

Startup companies do not have the budgets to devote to patents that large companies do, and that makes the business purpose of the patent portfolio even more important than that of their big competitors.

The key things for a startup's portfolio strategy are to forecast where the market may go and which competitors may be a problem, and then build the portfolio to address those issues. As those issues arise, spread a few patent resources around to put the company in a better position. As those resources bear fruit, repeat the process in a methodical way.

1.5.4 Business Does Not Have to Spend a Fortune on Patents

Large companies spend about 1% of their research and development budget on patent protection. Companies in the earlier stages of a high growth market typically spend more than 1%.[30]

Startups need to have an appropriate and meaningful patent strategy that does not waste money but is strong enough to be commercially useful.

---

29   April 2012, AOL sold 800 patents and granted a license to 300 more to Microsoft for a price of $1.056B. Facebook purchased about 650 of these patents from Microsoft for $550M (and we can assume that Microsoft kept licenses for itself on the patents that went to Facebook). See http://www.wired.com/2012/04/microsoft-aol-facebook/.

30   See "Patent Portfolios: Quality, Creation, and Cost" by Larry M. Goldstein, page 147, Table 3-5.

The amount to spend depends on the situation and the promise or potential of the company.

For an individual invention, a best practice is to wait not just until the technology risk, but most importantly, the business risk of an idea appears to be worth the investment.

For an entire portfolio, a best practice is to map out the business uses for patents during the company's timeline. At the appropriate stages, the company should pick the best available invention at that time to build up a portfolio.

1.6 A Business Purpose for Each Patent

The startup operates in a different world than big companies, especially when it comes to patents.

Large companies have enormous patent budgets that may pay for hundreds or even thousands of patents. The in-house attorneys at the big companies triage thousands of inventions each year, and may manage a docket of several hundreds of patents. They spend literally only minutes deciding which inventions to patent and which not to.

Startups are different. Each patent is a sizeable investment and worthy of a meaningful analysis.

When a startup decides to file a patent, that patent should meet at least one strong business goal and maybe several secondary goals. For example, a patent designed to keep competitors from directly competing may have outbound licensing potential as well as elements that may be cross licensed with another company.

Large companies can afford to spend a few of their budgeted patents for specific, targeted uses, but startups need to keep their options as open as possible.

Keep in mind that in almost every case, the business purpose of a patent will change over time. It may start out as a patent to keep out infringers but may wind up being cross licensed five or ten years later.

The key point: a startup should have a business purpose for each patent they file and that business purpose should justify the due diligence and extra time to do the patent well. Startups cannot afford to churn out high volumes of patents and hope that one of them might be valuable.

1.7 Common Mistakes That Startups Make

Startups make a lot of mistakes when it comes to patents. Some are due to inexperience, but many are due to poor advice.

One of the most common pieces of advice given to startups is to file a provisional application. This is some of the worst advice possible.

Provisional patent applications waste a startup's most precious asset: time.

The purpose of provisional patent applications is to <u>delay</u> the patent process. This is great for Big Pharma, where the value of their patent comes at the end of the patent term, but this is not the case for startups. [31]

Startups can get incredible amount of value from an issued patent, not just in raising the next round of investment. Many startups are able to license their technology to do all sorts of deals, such as having a vendor make an investment in exchange for a limited license to some technology.

Startup companies typically need patents fast.

Startup companies operate on a very short time horizon. They have a short runway, maybe 18 months, to reach certain goals and get to their next big milestone. Often, the next milestone is becoming revenue positive or another round of financing. Startups are not concerned about a 20 year lifespan of a patent—at least not in the early growth phase. They are just trying to live to see another day.

There are several techniques—the best of which is called the *Patent Prosecution Highway*—that can usually get a patent in 9-12 months.

---

31   A quirk of US patent law is that non-provisional applications have a patent life of 20 years from the date of filing. However, by filing a provisional application first, then filing a non-provisional a year later, the patent will be in effect until year 21.

Startups can get a lot of value out of a patent that issues quickly.

An issued patent gives the startup a huge leg up on meeting their milestones. They have cachet in the marketplace and a negotiating card to play with competitors. They also have a strong argument for why their company should have a much higher valuation, thereby making it easier to raise funds in each funding round.

Inventors who file their own patents are their own worst enemy.

Some inventors write their own patent applications. These applications are damaging in two ways.

One mistake is to disclose inventions that are purely conceptual. The half-baked discussion of an invention will come back to haunt them in three or four years when they file another patent on the fully-disclosed version of the invention.

The other mistake is to over-disclose information that has no business being in an invention disclosure. Often, the inventor will tell the world their entire business plan and the details of their technology, harming the company more than it helps.

Startups tend to cut corners on patents because of their lack of cash.

Sadly, most startup companies resort to strategies like provisional applications and other "cost-reducing" strategies that only delay their patents and actually add to the cost. CEOs often will not be able to justify the big initial investment in a patent at an early stage.

Further, expediting the patent will compress all of the patent costs into a very short period of time. Given that the average lifetime cost for a US patent is nearly $60,000, that is a huge investment.

Startups have a huge cost of capital.

Compounding the problem for the startup is that their capital costs are astoundingly high. The cost of capital raises the stakes even higher on whether or not to invest expensive capital on a patent.

If done well, the patent is likely to be the single most valuable asset for a young startup company, yet this book outlines countless ways that the asset could be worthless. By saving a couple dollars here or there, the entire value of the company can be decimated.

Because of the value of the patent assets to the company, there is no excuse not to do it well.

1.8 Own or Rent? Exclusive Licenses Can be More Valuable Than Owning Patents Outright

Patents encapsulate the hopes and dreams of a company and many investors, CEOs, and inventors have a negative gut reaction about not "owning" their patents. For some reason, "owning" their patents is a deeply emotional issue, but it should not be.

Sophisticated investors recognize the benefits of exclusive licenses and many prefer exclusive licenses over the cost, hassle, and uncertainty of having a startup manage its own patent portfolio.

Exclusive licenses are regularly done by universities and other technology transfer offices, as well as by patent holders and patent finance companies. These agreements are the way technologies can be moved into the marketplace without burdening a startup company and while giving the patent owner participation in the success.[32]

A licensor will grant an exclusive license when it wants another company to bring a technology to market. The exclusivity gives the licensee the incentive to invest in developing the market potential of the technology.

In contrast, a non-exclusive license dis-incentivizes the licensee from investing in developing a market. This is because the licensor could sell licenses to all of the company's competitors after the first licensee educates and cultivates the market for the product.

For a startup, having an exclusive license to a patent is actually more valuable than "owning" a patent.

Patents are a big capital investment for a startup company, but so is an office building. However, no startup company owns their office building outright. Even if they did own the building, they would take a mortgage on the building to free up capital. Exclusive licenses are the same thing as a lease agreement: the startup has full

---

32 Startups themselves may use exclusive licenses to give suppliers, vendors, competitors, or complementary businesses certain rights. An exclusive license may be narrowly focused, such as giving exclusive rights in a certain industry or geography.

control of the assets, but does not have to spend capital to build or maintain the asset.

1.8.1 An Exclusive License Aligns Incentives

In a licensing agreement, the licensee and licensor have aligned incentives. Both parties want the licensee to be successful.

The patent holder has every incentive to have a good patent.

The patent holder's only stock in trade is a quality patent. If the licensee cannot find any commercial value in the patent, the deal never gets done. It is incumbent on the patent holder to provide and maintain the highest quality patent possible.

Many licensing organizations, such as a select few of the major universities, have professional patent management systems in place. They professionally curate inventions and manage their portfolio to maximize the value to their licensees. [33]

When this is done well, the licensee startup company can benefit from professional patent management systems that they otherwise could not afford. Further, the licensor is incentivized to invest in the patents by paying for expedited costs, the additional costs for going up on appeal with the Patent Office, assistance in defending the patent from reexamination, or other costs that the startup can avoid.

1.8.2 An Exclusive License Eliminates Unpredictable Patent Costs

From a purely financial standpoint, an exclusive license reduces immediate patent costs and makes the costs predictable and manageable.

For a startup, unpredictable costs make for very difficult decisions. Should the CEO spend $4,000 on an office action response for the patent, or have a booth at a startup conference to attract investors? Which of these expenses will have the best return on investment

---

33   Sadly, most university technology transfer offices are woefully incompetent and do a very poor job. This is due to the fact that few understand the needs of the startup companies that the serve, as well as very poor internal incentives to close license deals.

for the company in the short term? Which expenses would be best in the long term?

In the analogy of owning the office building, a startup might be faced with an emergency roof repair, a plugged drain the bathroom, or repaving the parking lot. The unpredictable nature means that capital needs to be set aside to deal with the variability.

Unpredictable costs, such as patent costs, are managed by keeping a prudent reserve. The reserve can be managed explicitly, such as setting aside so many dollars for patent costs, or may be reactionary, where there is a churn of unpredictable expenses.

The prudent reserve—no matter how prudent—is still capital that cannot be deployed to grow the business. The more costs that can be predicted, the fewer reserves need to be set aside for the unpredictable costs, and the more capital can be fully deployed to advance the business.

1.8.3 Cost of Capital: Exclusive Licenses Make Financial Sense

When capital is scarce, it is very expensive. Most startups are capital constrained to the point where they sell off huge chunks of equity in exchange for small amounts of cash. In fact, most angel and venture backed capital comes with a cost of capital on the order of 40% per year.[34]

With the capital costs outrageously high, it makes sense to pay as little as possible and still control an asset. This arrangement leverages someone else's investment for the benefit of the company.

License fees are expenses and not an asset that needs to be capitalized.

Patent assets are often capitalized over 20 years, which is the lifetime of the assets. When a portfolio company pays a license fee, that fee is a direct expense and is not capitalized. Not only is the license

---

34   "Pepperdine Private Capital Markets Project, 2013 Capital Markets Report". Cost of capital of venture capital: 38.2%, private equity: 25.0%, mezzanine funding: 18.5%, asset backed loans: 13.0%, and banks: 6.8%. Report available at: http://cerescom.net/index. php?page=valuing-private-businesses-2013.

fee less than they would have paid initially, but those fees come directly off the bottom line.

1.8.4 Operationally, Exclusive Licenses Can Give a Company More Flexibility

Most exclusive licenses allow a licensee to modify the arrangement at any time. Most agreements allow the licensee to terminate the agreement by merely not paying the license fees, while other agreements might have other ways of changing the agreements.

A startup company may change focus, pivot, regroup, or find itself in a new market where their first patents are not useful. With a license agreement, the startup can often change the agreement without severe financial impact.

For example, an exclusive license agreement for a set of patents may allow the startup company to eliminate one or more patents from the agreement to reduce its costs. The licensor is taking a risk in that agreement, but giving the licensee more flexibility.

Many exclusive licenses allow for sublicensing.

Some exclusive licenses provide the option to sublicense the technology to another company.[35] Because the startup company has the exclusive license, the startup can often perform *outbound licensing*, such as sublicensing to competitors or spinout companies. This gives a startup company virtually the same business options as it would have had if they owned the patents outright.

Licensing agreements can have very creative payment arrangements.

Some license agreements may have different payment terms for different uses of the patents. For example, a university license agreement may include one percentage of gross revenues to be paid for products sold by the company but a different percentage for revenue received from sublicensing.

The allowable uses of the assets and the payments associated with those uses can be negotiating points when taking a license. The key

---

35   Not all exclusive licenses provide for sublicensing or cross-licensing options. Sometimes, these provisions can be limiting to a startup company, while other times not. It is important to know what restrictions—if any—come with the license agreement.

for the startup licensee would be to determine their likely usage scenarios of the assets first, then negotiate favorable terms for the most important uses of the assets.

Many companies or universities that license technologies to startups can have very favorable terms for startups. For example, a startup may be able to negotiate zero payments for a period of time yet may still have the full control of the assets during that time. As the startup becomes profitable or meets certain milestones, the payment terms may change to still be affordable.

Many license agreements are transferrable.

Many license agreements are transferrable to another company, such as an acquiring company. Transferrable licenses can be just as valuable—if not more—than transferring the patents in some situations.

Other license agreements may terminate on certain events, such as the licensee itself being sold. Often, such agreements may provide that the acquiring company may take a license under the same terms as the first licensee, which effectively makes the license transferrable.

Some licenses are not transferrable. These can pose unwanted restrictions on a startup's ability to exit, so these terms should be negotiated carefully.

1.8.5 License Arrangements Make a Company Immune to Lawsuits

An interesting side benefit of having patents in a separate entity is that the operating company is much less exposed to lawsuits.

Operating companies face many legal risks, from employment-related lawsuits to product liability lawsuits.

When patents are held in a separate company with separate control, a judgment from a lawsuit can never reach the patents. This means that a competitor, contractor, customer, employee, business partner, or anyone else cannot sue the company and hope to win the patents. This structure significantly reduces the attractiveness of the company from a plaintiff's standpoint.

Exclusive patent licenses are well known and respected throughout industry.

Many startup companies and CEOs do not have direct experience with exclusive or non-exclusive licenses, but these types of agreements are well respected and enforceable.

A license agreement is merely a contract. In the contract, each party can spell out their terms for what they receive and what they give in return. The license agreement can contain provisions such as arbitration clauses, mechanisms to rectify late payments, and all sorts of other terms.

Because license agreements are contracts, they can be negotiated, drafted, and reviewed by conventional contracts attorneys and enforced in local state court. This makes the costs relatively manageable.

2   How Startups Use Patents

Patents can be used in many different ways, and in this chapter, several possibilities are explained.

This chapter is not a comprehensive list of every way a patent can be used, and merely provides several examples to show the breadth of potential patent use.

Patents are business tools.

A CEO needs to be cognizant of how patents can help the business and be able to deploy patents effectively in negotiating deals with competitors, suppliers, customers, and investors.

The ways startups use patents can be thought of falling into two major categories: protecting the business and multiplying the business. In a protecting mode, patents protect an investor's capital by ensuring more operating room for the company and therefore higher margins. In a multiplying mode, the patents transfer technology to other players, who invest their own capital.

Protecting the business is much more than suing competitors who infringe. It includes cross licensing to defend against inbound assertions, helping with employment issues, and protecting the classic "razor/razor blade" type businesses.

Multiplying the business is about outbound licensing, "franchising" the technology, spinning out technologies to new vertical markets, negotiating deals based on exclusivity, creating industry standards, and other uses.

Pending patent applications are not useful business tools.

Throughout this section, it should be remembered that issued patents are being discussed, not pending patent applications. Pending patent applications can be enforced—theoretically—but not practically.

In a startup business context, expediting a patent application through the examination process can make a lot of economic sense. Expediting a patent costs extra money and compresses the patent costs into a few months, rather than spreading them out over several years.[1] However, the business uses of the patents can justify the expense.

A best practice would be to identify those patent applications that might serve a business purpose in the short term and spend the extra effort to expedite those patent applications. Other patent applications may not be as commercially valuable in the short term and may not justify the expense for expediting.

Before diving into the day-to-day uses of a patent, every investor wants to know how patents will help their portfolio companies get acquired.

2.1 Getting Acquired

Getting acquired by a bigger company (or going public) is usually the goal of a startup company, especially one with investors. Angel or venture capital investors usually have zero return until an exit happens, which is either an acquisition or an initial public offering (IPO).

It should be noted that having a viable business is an important step in being acquired. Without a viable business that has a solid, tested product and a track record of sales, the value of the business is based on its potential, not real economic value.

This is exactly the same criteria that was discussed in Chapter 1 about patents: the patent only has value when the technology risk and the market risk are removed.

This chapter explains how patents can make the business more valuable in several different contexts, but keep in mind that a viable company with mediocre patents will be much, much more valuable than a failing business with very good patents.

Very good patents can have stand-alone value, but rarely in the startup context, mostly because of the timeframe of the startup. A startup company, by its very nature, is bringing a new product to market and often is plowing new ground to do so.

---

1   Expediting a patent application is discussed in Chapter 3.

The market has not yet accepted the startup's new innovation and probably does not even know it exists. This means that the likelihood that anyone is infringing a patent is close to zero.

Couple that with the fact that patents can take a long time to get through the Patent Office, and the likelihood that a startup is holding a patent with provable infringement is even smaller.

However, the patents represent *potential* value over the next 17 years[2] in a specific market. This speculative value of the patents can have enormous value to acquiring companies.

Pending patent applications have little value in an acquisition context.

Throughout this discussion of getting acquired, the only meaningful patent assets are issued patents. This is because issued patents have a defined scope that can be analyzed and valued.[3]

Pending applications are rarely considered valuable in an acquisition context and are sometimes given zero or even negative value. This is because there is a large risk that the patent application may never be granted and that the scope of any issued patent is unknown, also, there may be many tens of thousands of dollars yet to spend to get the patents through the patent office.

2.1.1 Getting Acquired by an Infringer[4]

An investment-grade patent is a very big stick in any negotiation. Any time that stick is wielded, the company on the other side of the negotiations will be considering whether it is cheaper to acquire the patent owner or continue negotiations.

---

2   Patents are enforceable for a minimum of 17 years from the date the patent issues.

3   This is one reason why expediting a patent can be a very powerful strategy in a company that plans a relatively quick exit. The typical patent may take 3-7 years before it issues, but an expedited patent can issue in 9-12 months. Expediting a patent using the Patent Prosecution Highway or Track One is explained in Chapter 3.

4   An "infringer" in this context includes a company that actually infringes a patent, but can also include any company that *plans* to infringe. This can be a company that plans on entering a market or sees where their product line might eventually overlap the patent.

The two concepts are meant to be interchanged in this discussion. However, remember that actual, provable infringement is a much more valuable incentive to be acquired than *possible* infringement that might happen in the future.

This type of acquirer knows or suspects that they might infringe a patent, and it may make financial sense to purchase the startup company outright rather than pay a license fee or have the threat of litigation. The startup company's valuation would include not only the value of the product and customers, but also the value of the patents from a strategic standpoint.

The strategic standpoint of the acquiring company can be to help clear out a defensible marketspace for future growth.

Part of a good due diligence analysis prior to filing a patent application can include analysis of companies who are acquiring patent assets in the same space as the startup company.

For example, the following screenshot from AcclaimIP shows the companies who are acquiring assets in the space of optical analysis of chemicals or materials:

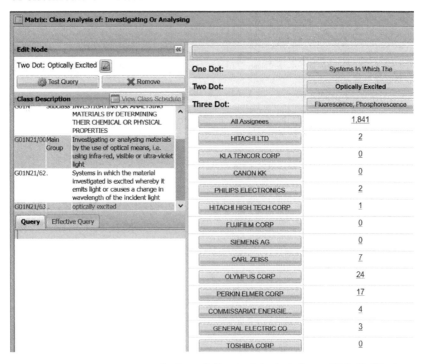

Figure 1 Patent Acquisitions in the Optical Chemical Analysis Space, CPC G01N21/00, data as of March 2016, courtesy of AcclaimIP.com. Used with permission.

From this analysis, we can see that Olympus Corp and Perkin Elmer have both made patent acquisitions in this space. For a startup in this space, both companies would be target acquirers.

But it does not stop there. The universe of acquiring companies is much larger.

2.1.2 Getting Acquired by a Non-Infringer

Patents are just as likely to be acquired by anyone who is in competition with or wants to do business with the infringer or potential infringer.

The enemy of my enemy is my friend.

Big companies that are in litigation with each other often go on a buying spree for patents that are infringed by the other party. These patents might have nothing to do with the purchasing company's business but have value purely because someone else infringes the patent.

Patents purchased in the heat of litigation can be very expensive to the purchaser because of the imminent threat, but companies often purchase patents for possible cross licensing or other negotiation with a competitor.

This opens up a much larger pool of possible acquirers than just the anticipated infringer.

Any company who competes with the infringer would be interested in the patent, even if the company competes in a completely different space. In this case, the patent might be relatively useless to the acquiring company except in the situation where it can negotiate with the infringer. A typical negotiation may result in cross-licensing or some other agreement.

But the universe of acquirers is even bigger than competitors to the infringer.

Virtually any company who does business with the infringer, such as a supplier or customer, could use the infringed patent to negotiate a better deal with the infringer.

In all of these cases, the key to the patent value—and the likelihood of being acquired—comes from having strong, investment-grade patents. Weak, poorly written patents will not open up many of these acquisition opportunities.

2.2 Building a Moat Around the Business

When it comes to patents, CEOs often state that they want to defend their turf, but they rarely have a good picture of how that works. Often, the CEOs will follow on by saying that they would not have the ability to defend their patents anyway, and they quickly run out of reasons to have patents.

There is much more to defending a company's turf than going to court to enforce a patent, but few startup CEOs know how it all works.

Patents can be asserted in two broad scenarios: thieves who flat out copy technology, and competitors who build something close but not exact. Most people understand how patents work in the first instance, but often not in the second.

The second mouse gets the cheese.

The second mover in a market gets the advantage of all of the startup's hard work. The startup thrashes around figuring out what actually works, educates the consumer about the actual product, then begins to get traction. Once that ground is plowed, which is very slow going at first, a competitor can breeze right in with the advantage of everything the startup taught them.

The patent is one way to have that competitor either cease and desist or pay a license to use the technology. The patent gives the startup leverage to have a legitimate, legal business discussion with a competitor.

2.2.1 Enforcing Patents Against Direct Copiers

Patents are incredibly valuable when there are direct copies of a product. A very real scenario is when a startup hires an unscrupulous foreign manufacturer who runs two shifts a day making product that they send to the startup and a third shift of product that they sell out the back door.

A software company may have product that is downloaded and resold under another brand, or they may have a disgruntled employee that walks out the door with source code only to pop up at a competitor the next day.

Both of these scenarios can be handled by patent enforcement.

Patents can be enforced without going to court.

Enforcing a patent in these situations is not the multi-million dollar ordeals that we read about in the news.

At the Consumer Electronics Show in Las Vegas, startups routinely enforce their patents by shutting down exhibitors who have knock off products. The Consumer Electronics Association fully supports these actions, and startups have shown up at a competitor's booth armed with a handful of patents (and an official from CES), and had exhibitors take down infringing products as they watched.

In another scenario, a relatively small patent holder sent a letter to a very small business who was manufacturing a competing product that may or may not have infringed. The patent holder was able to negotiate a cash payment and require that the small business change their product design. The patent holder allowed the small business to sell off their holiday inventory, but the small business ceased being a direct competitor.

The International Trade Commission is an agency of the federal government that has the power to stop inbound shipments as they enter the United States. The ITC is the best place to assert patents and stop competitors from importing infringing patents. The cost to assert patents in this forum is quite modest, and they act very quickly.

In all three of these examples, patent holders are able to make enormous impacts in protecting their business without large cash investments.

One of the biggest factors in the success or failure of these types of enforcement actions is the quality of the patent. A startup company will get much more favorable results when they are asserting very high quality patents.[5]

2.2.2 Enforcing Patents by Going to Court

Conventionally, patents are enforced by going to court—or seriously threatening to do so. This is often a big monetary commitment, to the tune of $5 million.

When there are tens of millions of dollars at stake, there are many groups that will take these cases on a contingency fee. These include law firms but also include private companies. They will bring lawsuits against big companies,and they have the resources for seeing the lawsuits to the end.

Most lawsuits are a big game of chicken and never actually get to court. Each side postures and pushes the other side around, hoping that the other side will back down and negotiate first. Typically, both sides want to negotiate, but the lawsuit devolves into a huge process of wearing the other one down. If one side does not have the money to bring the case to completion, the other side will wear them down and will outspend them until they give up.[6]

Because the cost of a lawsuit is so extraordinarily high, it only makes business sense in cases where there is $50 million at stake--or more.

2.2.3 Defending an Investment in Other Situations

Patents are business assets. In some situations, they are just like trading cards.

---

5 In this context, a high quality patent is merely one that is readable and understandable. The easier it is for an infringer to simply read and understand the patent, the smoother these enforcement actions will go. Patents that are written in twisted, convoluted legalese are much, much harder to assert because the infringer must get their lawyers involved to decipher the patent.

6 Companies in Silicon Valley and elsewhere have been taking the position that they will not even look at another company's patents and negotiate a reasonable license. This is in response to their hatred of so-called patent trolling.

This shortsighted and damaging practice actually compounds the patent trolling problem. Legitimate patent owners must now employ patent trolls to file lawsuits just so that they can open discussions. Rather than settling on a royalty that a patent holder might think is reasonable (maybe $100K), they go to court for tens of millions.

In a competitive technology field, it is highly likely that a startup will step on someone else's technology and their patent. It may be directly, such as when the core product infringes, or it may be tangentially, where a product might use patented technology as an enabling technology.

In either situation, someone might send a letter implying that the startup infringes their patent. They could be forceful and demand that the startup cease and desist, or they could kindly suggest that the startup take a license to their patent. This is where cross-licensing can come into play.

A cross license is where a startup and the other patent owner agree to let each other use their patents. Often, one side might pay the other side a royalty, but it would be a much smaller royalty than if there were no patent rights going along with it.

Many companies have big patent portfolios purely for cross licensing. Lots of competing companies have formal cross license agreements in place. Microsoft and Apple had such a deal that was part of Microsoft's cash investment in Apple in the 1980's. This deal allowed Apple to avoid bankruptcy, but it also gave Microsoft access to Apple's user interface technology.

Many giant companies have monumentally big portfolios that serve as a "silent cross license" with other companies. These companies are staring across No Man's Land at each other from their foxholes, each with a huge pile of weapons waiting for the patent Armageddon. Microsoft and Google have been in this pose for over a decade, and it remains to be seen if that ever happens.

2.2.4 Getting Access to Someone Else's Patented Technology by Writing a Patent

When a company wants to use someone else's patented technology, one very good way is to file their own patent in the same space.

Of course, a patent cannot be granted on something that someone else has already disclosed, but there are always patents that can be written on a piece that may be missing from the existing patent or the next logical step for where the market will go.

The sequence will go like this:

Let's say a competitor has a patent on an airplane. The claims require:

- An engine
- A propeller
- A wing

A startup invents the biplane, which is novel (never been done before) and non-obvious (having two wings gives better performance and structural integrity). The patent office awards a patent with claims:

- An engine
- A propeller
- At least two wings

The startup clearly infringes the competitor's patent, because the biplane has every element of their patent. But now the startup can stop the first company from building biplanes. The startup now has something to trade or cross license with its competitor.

Rather than negotiating a license fee for the airplane patent from a competitor, the startup can cross license the biplane patent. Maybe the startup can even negotiate for the first company to pay when they build biplanes, if the biplanes become more popular than the regular airplanes.

The point of this scenario is that even though someone else holds a patent in a startup's space, there is still room to invent improvements and sell or license them back to the original patent holder.

2.2.5 Patents and Open Source Software

Open source software is not often protected by patents, which is unfortunate. However, there are situations where patents are particularly valuable.

In a commercial open source software context, a company may release its code open source but may place restrictions on use. A company may, for example, allow educational and non-commercial use of its products but may charge for commercial use.

A patent portfolio can be used to enforce the commercial-use restrictions of the software while allowing the code to be freely available to the public.

2.2.6 Protecting a Razor Blade Business

Many businesses have the razor/razor blade model, where they sell one product at a lower cost (sometimes free) with the hope that they sell replacement parts or consumables.

Patents play a very big role in protecting this business model.

Patents are great for protecting interfaces, mechanical and otherwise. The interfaces may be an application programming interface (API) in the software area, or it may be an electrical communication protocol in an internet-of-things product, or it may be a mechanical connection for a razor blade.[7]

In general, these patents have very little stand-alone value, but they will prevent anyone from building a product that connects to the interface. With patents on the interface, the patent owner can license the patents to other companies to make products that connect to the product.

This licensing scenario allows the company to certify and approve each vendor. Some companies can arrange a deal so that a third party pays for "certification" as well as paying a license fee per unit sold.

These patents are typically narrow and rather specific, so they do not have much value outside of the specific product's ecosystem, but inside the ecosystem, they allow the owner to control how products will grow and still get a piece of the action.

2.2.7 Protecting any As-A-Service Business

Many companies operate "as-a-service." In the software space, there are companies that provide authentication services or payment

---

7   Design patents can be especially effective for protecting mechanical interfaces. Design patents are much more cost effective than utility patents, and typically cost $3000-5000, compared to $56,000+ for utility patents.

services. In the physical products space, there are companies that provide manufacturing or fulfillment services. In the financial services space, companies will provide background checks or other services.

In each of these cases, the business model is to take previously known functions or services and specialize. The specialization allows a customer to build their business without having to build their own authentication platform or fulfillment center.

The "as-a-service" business can be protected by patents on the interfaces, because competitors will have to have the same or similar interfaces.

There are several interfaces for any "as-a-service" business. These include the normal customer interface as well as various administrative interfaces.

For example, an authentication-as-a-service business might have an API through which a website may direct a user to the service, and once authentication was completed, the API may transmit a token. This may be the interface to the customer. A second interface may be an administrative user interface or API that provides analytics for how often the service was used, its success or failure rate, and other data. A third interface may be a configuration interface that a customer uses to set up and install the service as well as perform maintenance or change services.

Patentable business advantages may be found on each of these interfaces, and these patents will give the company a distinct advantage in controlling the market, either by excluding other competitors or licensing their interface technology to other providers.

2.2.8 Dealing With Employment Issues

A company-wide strategy for patents can have ancillary benefits when dealing with employee issues.

For example, a company that operates in a highly competitive market for talent can use its patent portfolio to limit the damage when employees leave and work at a competitor.

Documenting and reviewing inventions is a best practice.

The company's practices of periodically reviewing patentable aspects of the business set the tone that the company is aware of its trade secrets and their value. This has a benefit of putting employees on notice that there is value in the intellectual property.

Such a company may regularly document its progress by filing patents, which legally document the inventions owned by the company.

The employees know the technologies that are owned by the company because they were listed as inventors on a patent and are much less likely to repeat the same invention when they jump to a competitor. Further, the competitor does not want a patent fight to ensue, so that competitor may look less favorably at poaching talent from the company.

Filing a patent after an inventor leaves the company.[8]

When a key employee leaves the company, the company might wish to file a patent on anything that the employee was working on at the end of their tenure. With some of the recent changes to the patent law, the company can easily file the patent in the name of the inventor who left the company, but only when there is an employee agreement that transfers any inventions to the company.

In a typical scenario, a patent might be written within a month or two of the employee's termination.[9] The former employee will be sent the paperwork to sign.[10]

---

8   At first glance, this might be counterintuitive. Often, a startup company—especially a very early startup—will have key founders that disagree and leave the company. The first response might be to file a patent application without the founder who left, but this can invalidate the patent due to improper inventorship. Inventorship issues are further discussed in Chapter 4.

9   This timeframe is just an example. It is best to write this patent application as quickly as possible, but sometimes the patent application might be written a year or more after the inventor left the company.

10   The paperwork would include a letter stating that the patent application and all related information are company secrets and protected under the former employee's agreement with the company. This would prevent the employee from sharing the patent application with their new employer.

The former employee might refuse to sign, and the startup would then file the patent anyway and the employee is put on notice about what is owned by the company.

One big benefit of doing this is to eliminate *inventorship* problems down the road.

The former employee might refuse to sign the paperwork and state that they were not an inventor which prevents them from creating an improper inventorship problem later. This would invalidate the patent.

When the former employee does sign the agreement, they are agreeing that the assets are owned by their previous employer, thereby heading off another potential problem.

This can prevent their new employer from using the trade secrets from their new employee without potentially incurring liability.

A side benefit of these practices is that other companies might be less inclined to poach talent from the startup.

2.3 Multiplying an Investment with Patents

The best patents are those that multiply an investment and actually generate money on their own.

Some companies have devolved into purely research and development companies that license technology. The integrated circuit industry has almost completely changed to this model, where integrated circuit chips are designed in house, but the fabrication is done exclusively at third party foundries.

Some companies invested in technologies but make more money licensing their technology to competitors. Microsoft famously makes more money licensing their patents to Android competitors than it does manufacturing and selling their own mobile phones.

These are some ways the Fortune 100 handle their patent portfolios, and the same principles apply to startups.

The patent creates a multiplier effect to an investment.

A patent allows the startup to license—and control—additional delivery vehicles for their product. The delivery vehicle can be:

- a direct competitor who takes a license;

- a spin out company that applies the product to another market or vertical;

- a franchisee who invests their own capital to replicate the business plan in another location or market; or

- a standards body that adopts the solution to a problem, then licenses it across hundreds of manufacturers.

The patent is the mechanism by which technology is transferred to different lines of business, some of which the startup might control directly, and some of which someone else might fund and control. In any event, these mechanisms are the gifts that keep on giving.

2.3.1 Outbound Licensing into other Verticals

Startup companies never have enough resources to attack all of the markets they want to enter, so why not have other people do some of that work?

A startup should be entering the markets that are easiest for them. Maybe the founder has experience in one end of the market, or the chosen market has the lowest barrier to entry. However, there are always more markets to attack than there are resources.

Many startup CEOs can lose sight of the other markets for their product. For example, a company may be attacking the high volume, low cost end of the market, but there may be lots of opportunity in the low volume, high value end as well.

If a company is positioned as the high volume leader, it may not translate well to the high value end. Maybe it makes sense to either spin out a separate brand as a wholly-owned subsidiary or to license the technology to a company already addressing the higher end of the market.

In either scenario, the patents are the mechanism by which the rights to the technology are transferred.[11] A license agreement may specify which markets they can enter and which markets they might need to leave alone. For some technologies, the wider they are adopted, even at a very modest or even no license fee, the better it might be for a business.

2.3.2 Franchising Solutions to Others

One of the best ways to expand a brand is through franchising. In a franchise model, another entrepreneur gets the benefit of all the investment a startup entrepreneur made in building a business, then builds their own business on top of it.

A franchise can be a branded business, such as a conventional restaurant franchise, but could also be a business that operates in a different market. The other market may be geographical or a different vertical.

The key to a franchise model is that there is a separate business that pays a license fee to the patent owner, who is the licensor. The licensor controls the actions of the franchisee in order to preserve the branding and other goodwill that the franchise includes, and the patents allow the licensor to enforce the agreements.

2.3.3 Spinning Out Technologies

A company solves many problems on their way to bringing a product to market. The solutions to these problems are often things that other companies will also have to solve.

Products that address these secondary problems are excellent candidates for spinning out businesses to further develop the technology. These spin out companies can be wholly-owned subsidiaries or have separate ownership. Like with franchising, the technology gets transferred to a spin out company by a license to the patents.

---

11   In most of these types of outbound licensing deals, there may be trade secrets, ways of doing business, branding, and other intellectual property that is licensed, but the patents are often the only legally enforceable right that can be exercised to enforce the entire license contract.

2.3.4 Negotiating With Suppliers

The type of business deals that can be done with patents are virtually endless; one example is an agreement made with suppliers.

A vendor may manufacture a product for a startup. The startup, having little money but having a patent, may negotiate a limited license agreement with the vendor.

For example, a vendor may wish to add the startup's product to their product line. A startup may negotiate a limited exclusive license that would allow the vendor to sell the product in a specific vertical market, and the vendor will invest capital to build a manufacturing plant.

The license agreement may give the vendor a right to enter a market that the startup was not even considering, and may include an agreement that the vendor will produce samples or production quantities for the startup to sell in a different vertical market.

In such a deal, the patents are the only item pledged by the startup, but in return the vendor pledges a capital contribution along with some services.

2.3.5 Standards Essential Patents

The holy grail of patents is a "standards essential" patent, where the technology is baked into standardized products. Virtually all of the standard computer and network interfaces are licensed under patent pools.

Standards essential patents are often worth tens of millions of dollars or more, but even more importantly, owners of the standards essential patents get a seat at the table of the patent pool. They can strongly influence how the standards evolve, which can be even more valuable.

Patent enforcement has been a part of the landscape since the days of the mechanical sewing machine in the mid-1800s. There were a handful of essential patents that stopped a group of infringing companies from proceeding. A patent pool was created called the

Sewing Machine Combination to license seven essential patents to the industry.

Since then, notable patent pools were formed by the Wright Brothers and Curtiss Company in airplanes, color TVs in the 1960's, and many others. Today's technologies such as JPEG, MPEG, Bluetooth, virtually all IEEE standards, and many other industry standards are all licensed through patent pools.

Today's patent pools are highly organized groups where patent holders submit their patents and a licensing organization grants licenses, collects a royalty, and disburses payments according to the value of the patents to the standard. These pools are open to any patent holder, including startup companies and independent inventors, but largely are run by giant corporations that design patent portfolios just for this purpose.

Standards essential patents are the holy grail of patents in today's business landscape.

Most startups are focused on getting a product to market quickly, getting validation, and starting a revenue stream. Once there, the startups begin to scale.

If there is any chance that a startup's technology—even a piece of it—could be incorporated into an industry standard, the patent needs to be investment-grade. In these situations, multiple patents would also be a good investment.

2.4 Patents Get Horse-Traded on a Sophisticated Secondary Market

A very sophisticated and extremely well financed secondary market for patents lies behind a thick veil of secrecy. Most entrepreneurs and investors (and even most patent attorneys) are unaware of this market and how it works.

The secondary patent market is usually where so-called patent trolls come out from under their bridges to launch lawsuits to assert patents.[12]

12   In many cases, so-called patent trolls are the best friend of independent inventors and small businesses. Big companies are usually not that innovative, so they wind up

The secondary patent market is much more advanced than people realize, and this market is yet one more of the many audiences for patents.

2.4.1 The Secondary Patent Market Has Exploded in the Last Two Decades

The secondary patent market now includes patent aggregators, patent assertion companies, "catch-and-release" syndications, auction-based sales, a big group of independent patent brokers, and many others. There are sophisticated insurance policies that protect against many different patent-related business scenarios. There is even a professional society for the industry, the Licensing Executives Society, which has nearly 3,000 members in the US and Canada.

Most of the companies in the secondary patent market are privately held, although some are publicly listed. At last count, there were 20 or more public companies whose primary business was patent enforcement or licensing.

Often, these companies get started with a lucky win early on, which they try to duplicate over and over. Some get stronger, some fail, but they all quickly morph over time. Although these companies get bad press, they tend to do business in the hundreds of millions-and sometimes billions-of dollars.

The secondary patent market is rarely the first thought of an inventor when the lightbulb goes off, but it is a very good mechanism for unloading patent assets that a company might not be using. Take for example a venture backed company that has—to use a polite term—"pivoted" at some stage in the game.

There may be patents that the company is no longer using but still owned. These patents can be liquidated, either through a one-time sale or through ongoing licensing, to other people in the market. Sometimes, the startup will keep a license to the technology; sometimes not.

---

copying technologies once someone else proves that it can work, but the big companies do not want to pay for it.

The secondary market for patents is notoriously secretive and has a cloak and dagger feel to it. This is because there are lots of veiled (and not-so-veiled) threats being made, and lots of very hard negotiations. Almost all of the deals are signed with strict confidentiality agreements, and we only get a glimpse when publically traded companies reveal these deals in SEC or other mandatory disclosure filings.

2.4.2 Why all the Secrecy?

The cloak-and-dagger aspects to this market are an artifact of the legal system. If someone formally accuses a company of patent infringement, the company can use the accusation to run to court and get a declaratory judgment to invalidate the patent. This is known in the industry as getting "DJ-ed." To avoid the declaratory judgment, the patent owner has to make the veiled threat without actually being threatening—or—the patent owner must file the lawsuit first in their own jurisdiction, then tell the infringer afterwards, which comes across as aggressive.[13]

Consequently, people on the receiving end often get notice of the lawsuit completely out of the blue, which causes them to angrily complain about "patent trolls." It is ironic that the declaratory judgment law was put in place to help alleged infringers ward off lawsuits, but in practice actually makes it much more difficult for the alleged infringers.

---

13 This is one reason why the term "infringement" is not often used in the secondary patent market. The polite term is "evidence of use."

3   Managing the Process

Managing the patent process is relatively straightforward, so long as a plan is in place.

The plan comes from due diligence analysis prior to filing a patent. The plan includes the business aspects of the invention that are important and serves as a reference guide for the patent attorney during the examination process, as well as a reference for determining whether or not the original business and technical assumptions of the patent remain valid.

3.1 A Repeatable Due Diligence Analysis Prior to Filing

The decision to file a patent is an investment that—if it pays off—will have a huge benefit to a company. The best way to ensure that the decision process is well thought out is to have a due diligence process that helps make the decision less emotional and more quantifiable.

The due diligence is a roadmap for the business case of the patent and needs to follow the patent through its lifecycle.

The due diligence analysis should consolidate and organize the thought processes and data underlying the business decision for a patent.

One piece of the analysis can include the invention checklist, which is described in Chapter 4.

The due diligence should include some preliminary economic analysis of the invention. The due diligence should determine if the invention is a $3 improvement to a $10 product, or if it is a $0.03 improvement to a $1,000 product.

All of the due diligence practices should remove emotion and "gut feel" from the decision making process. Far too many patents are pursued to reward an inventor for a job well done or because the invention was "cool," and not for the dollars and cents that might come of the investment.

The due diligence process is an iterative process. A checklist might be used to triage an invention and determine whether or not to investigate further, but then a thorough patent search should be performed.

The patent search may uncover related patents that would severely narrow the scope of a patent for the invention being discussed. Once the patent search is performed, a set of patent claims should be constructed and the checklist applied again to determine whether or not to go forward to file a patent.

3.2 Focus on Quality First, Then Quantity

It has been said that patents are like hyenas. One hyena can be easily defeated, but not a whole pack.

When doing multi-million dollar patent negotiations, patent quantity is often more important than quality. A large number of patents, which may be 10 patents in some cases or 100 patents in others, have an air of invincibility. Maybe a competitor could try to take down one or two patents that might be infringed, but when there are too many patents, the cost equation goes the other way and it is easier to negotiate and settle.

A startup cannot afford an entire pack of hyenas, so it must focus on patents that can withstand attack on their own.

High quality patents only take one thing: a bit more hard work.

Startups may not have the resources to build big patent portfolios. However, they do have the resources to do high quality patents. High quality comes with a bit more hard work.

The hardest part of doing a quality patent is to not rush the due diligence: take the time to thoroughly research the best design around alternatives, hone in on the points of novelty, and think through the different ways the invention may be adopted by the market. The patent drafting should be deliberate and well thought out, and the examination process should be complete and thorough.

Startups often convey a breathless need for speed. Time is the enemy of a startup, but the difference between a weakly written, poorly thought out patent application and a well-researched one is monumental.

There are two pleasant side benefits of writing quality patent applications: they tend to cost less, and they tend to be granted faster.

As the startup grows, there may be areas where quantities of patents begin to make sense. Larger numbers of patents would be especially helpful in technologies where there may be litigation or outbound licensing.

3.3 Avoid Wishful Thinking Patents

Many patents are filed with "wishful thinking." This occurs when someone wants protection on a product but does not realize what the scope of the invention will actually be.

For example, let's say a company is making a fully automated, table top ice cream machine. Consumers will load up the machine with various ingredients, and the machine will process the ingredients into a fabulous frozen dessert. The CEO usually tells the patent attorney, "I want a patent on this." And the patent attorney goes to work.

There are plenty of ice cream machines on the market, from hand cranked or motor-assisted cranked machines to automated industrial-sized factories that produce the same basic product.

In order to get a patent, the patent claims may include an electronic scale for measuring ingredients and a chiller for pre-chilling liquid ingredients prior to processing.

The result is a patent on a table top machine with ingredient reservoirs, a scale that measures ingredients, and a pre-chilling system.

If a competitor were to build the same machine without the scale that measures ingredients, they would not infringe and the patent would not stop them. This might happen, for example, when a competitor's machine uses a pre-measured kit for frozen desserts, which might eliminate the need for the scale.

The CEO does not realize that even though their patent application describes all of the many elements of their product, the patent claims are actually very narrow and easy to design around. What the patent actually protects—from a legal standpoint—is much different than what it describes.

How to prevent this from happening.

The first way is to educate the CEO to help him or her understand what might actually be covered by the patent. In the example above, the CEO may have believed that the point of novelty was that the machine was fully automated. However, the true, legal point of novelty may have been the scale for measuring ingredients.

The CEO believed the patent would keep the semi-automated competitors out of the field and probably made critical business decisions based on that belief. However, the true point of novelty was merely the scale, and a design around analysis[1] would have uncovered both the narrowness of the claim and the opportunity for a new product line.

The CEO needs to know the protection afforded by the claims of the patent, not the description. The CEO should steer the company's business proposition to align with the patent claims (or vice versa).

When the CEO believes that their patent is much more broad than it really is, the company's marketing and product roadmap often wanders into unprotected territory. The result is that they build market and brand equity that is not reflected in their patent assets, which causes the patents to not have their intended value and causes the business to not to be able to use the patents effectively.

3.4 Getting Patents Fast

Most of the major patent offices of the world, including the USPTO, have programs for getting patents fast. A typical patent may move through the system over several years, and 3-7 years is pretty typical. However, these expedited programs can get the patent very quickly, sometimes within 9-12 months.

---

1 Design around analysis is discussed in Chapter 4. A design around analysis does not have to be expensive, but merely a thought experiment with the inventors or maybe some technical people.

The USPTO has three systems for expediting patents. The best system is called the Patent Prosecution Highway. The next preferred system is Track One, and the system called Accelerated Examination is so hopelessly crippled that nobody should ever use it.

Special Status

The USPTO has a "Special Status" for certain patents. Special Status is granted if the inventor is over 65 years old, as a courtesy to inventors who probably will not live to the end of their patent's expiration.[2]

With Special Status, the case is on the examiner's 10 day docket, and the examiner needs to process the case within 10 days. In comparison, the examiner's first action docket (where they pick up a case for the first time) can be three to five years long.

From the examiner's standpoint, Special Status tends to disrupt their examination rhythm and, when the Special cases take a long time, make it really hard to reach their production goals. In effect, examiners hate Special Status cases.

From the patent attorney's standpoint, Special Status is a powerful tool for negotiation. Examiners have extra incentive to move cases towards allowance so that the cases get off their irritating Special docket, and this provides an opportunity for the attorney to have a meaningful discussion with the examiner.

Couple the better negotiating position with the fact that the examiner must respond within two weeks on everything the attorney sends in, and patents will issue very quickly.

The expediting programs move a patent to Special Status.

All of the programs for expediting a patent application are ways to get Special Status.

In the case of Track One, the applicant merely pays a fee (typically in the range of $2,000-4,000) and the case is granted Special Status. The catch is that the applicant gets Special Status for only two Office

---

2   There are several other conditions in which the Office will grant Special Status, but most of these conditions require a written petition with supporting documents. The Office is notorious for taking so long to grant these petitions that the patents actually issue before the petition gets reviewed.

actions. If the case cannot be allowed in that time, the case goes back to normal status. [3]

With the Patent Prosecution Highway, the case is granted Special Status for the entire time it is at the USPTO. This includes going up on appeal. The Patent Prosecution Highway is the premier way of getting Special Status.

The Patent Prosecution Highway is a program where Special Status is granted when another patent-granting authority says that certain claims are allowable, which is the justification for Special Status. The fastest way to get this status is to file a Patent Cooperation Treaty (PCT) application. This international application is examined quickly, and an International Search Report is generated in 3-6 months.

The cost of a PCT application is about the same order of magnitude as the USPTO's Track One cost, yet the applicant cannot lose Special Status.

3.5 A Roadmap for a Startup's Portfolio

A startup's patent portfolio can be thought of in two distinct patent types: prophetic patents and non-prophetic. Non-prophetic patents can also be thought of as "data-driven" patents. Prophetic patents are a necessary evil, but they can be very damaging to a startup when used badly.

Prophetic patents are those that are almost purely forward-looking. These patents are filed prior to raising funds or at least before going to market. They are prophetic in the sense that there are guesses about how the technology will work and how the market will adopt the technology.

Non-prophetic or "data-driven" patents cover things for which data exists. The data may be performance-related test data, or market-related data that comes from customer behavior. The patents that come from market-related data tend to be some of the most valuable patents in a portfolio.

---

3   Usually, the longest wait time is for the first examination, which will come very quickly on Track One. The subsequent office actions, even if they are on normal status, will take 2-3 months to receive a response.

The idea of "data-driven" patents is that there is substantive data that supports the business proposition of the patent. The substantive data can be test results, but the most important data are market results. When the patent captures a deep market insight, such as a customer pain point, that patent has strong commercial value.

In general, data-driven patents will have much more value than prophetic patents for two reasons:

- There is less guesswork about the technology, which means the claims will be more meaningful.

- The decision to protect something has real business value, meaning the money is well spent.

The data-driven patents can also be thought of as risk-reduced patents. The risk of a patent is the technology risk and the market risk. When data exists on either the technology or market risk, the overall risk of a patent goes down.[4]

A startup needs prophetic patents at the very beginning to get started. These will protect the basic idea of the business's product, but it is critical to avoid creating downstream problems with these patents. As the startup grows, it will understand the markets better, and it will solve technical problems on the way to realizing its goal.

These two elements—understanding the markets and solving problems along the way—are where the real gems of a patent portfolio lie. However, these assumptions cannot be verified when the first patent is written. The discussion below provides solutions to handling this dilemma.

3.5.1 Filing the First Patent

The first patent is typically filed prior to entering the market. This prophetic patent might have several different ways a product may be designed and capture a couple different ways the product may go to market.

---

4   One of the fascinating aspects of patents is that they must have inherent risk. If all of the risks are removed, the invention becomes more "obvious" and it becomes more difficult to be allowed by the examiner. Every patent has to have an "inventive step" or "ah-ha moment."

At the point that the patent is filed, there are only guesses about how the market will respond. These guesses may be risk-reduced by doing market research, testing landing page conversions, or just talking with potential customers. However, the real market response comes when customers break out their credit cards and pay money for the product.

The purpose of the first patent application is to clear some space so that the company can keep competitors away. This patent application is done with the highest degree of uncertainty about both the technology and the market. It is critical to note that not only is the entrepreneur just beginning the journey at this point, but so is the patent attorney. Neither player knows which elements of the invention will turn out to be important.

The first patent will NOT be the most important patent in the portfolio, so do not treat it like it is.

Conceptually, the first patent might be merely a placeholder or framework into which other patents will follow. Practically, this patent application must capture the one or two points of novelty that differentiate the product—and nothing more.

The claiming strategy for the first patent should cover the points of novelty of the product as it will be introduced, and the claims should be somewhat broader than normal. The strategy is to get some feedback from the examiner (i.e., a rejection) and get a better lay of the land for what could be patented in this area.[5]

Do NOT put too much information in the first patent.

Far too many inventors and entrepreneurs file gigantic, self-written prophetic provisional applications. These are a very bad practice.

"Kitchen sink" patents—where everything is thrown in—can cause endless problems down the road. These patent applications are brain dumps of as much information as possible. Some people even copy

---

5   Often, this is done by having both relatively broad and relatively narrow claims. The narrow claims are designed to be allowed quickly, giving the startup a patent it can use for business, and the broad claims force the examiner to give a landscape of the allowable subject matter.

pages from their lab notebooks and stuff them into a provisional application, mistakenly thinking that somehow they are protected.

This is one of the worst practices.

Disclosing too much information prevents getting a patent on the actual invention when the research is actually invested to figure out how to do it. [6]

Everything in a patent application is prior art which will be used against the company down the road. This includes provisional applications, which are publically available once their non-provisional cousins become public.

When a provisional application states that something is possible but does not explain how to do it, an examiner can still cite it as prior art.

The scenario: An inventor of an artificial sponge product writes and files a "kitchen sink" provisional application and happens to mention that fibers could be included in the product. The inventor had a guess that fibers could be added, and the concept was on the long list of things to explore.

Three years later, there is a huge need in the market for stronger sponge products. In fact, several customers were offering to pay an enormous premium to have the stronger products.

So, the inventor tries adding fibers to the product. It turns out that adding fibers was very difficult, and there was a lot of development to determine how to distribute the fibers in suspension and how to keep the fibers in the product while it cures, and the length of fibers really made a big difference.

Proud of the accomplishment, the company submits a patent application for the fiber, unaware that there was a mere mention of the fibers in the original patent application.

---

6   See also Chapter 1, where the *quid pro quo* between the patent applicant and the government is discussed. Making unnecessary public disclosure of trade secrets is also damaging to the company.

The examiner rejects the claims stating: "The inventor said that it was possible to add fibers to the mix in the provisional application three years ago."

Now the company is stuck. They cannot argue with their original patent without weakening it completely, nor can they argue that their new patent application deserves broad coverage.

Even if the company is able to save the second patent by claiming priority to the first patent, the company loses all international rights to the second invention.[7]

The purpose of the first patent is to cover the "big" point of novelty of a business, but the next batch of patents are where the real protection begins. These are explained below.

3.5.2 Know What is Protected—And What is Not

Many CEOs mistakenly tell investors what they think their patent covers, and this can be very misleading. The easy way to tell is when the CEOs make excessively broad, sweeping statements about what their patents cover. In many cases, this is not because the CEO is being disingenuous or deceitful; it is because they do not understand this basic concept:

Patent protection comes from the <u>claims</u>, not from the <u>description</u>.

The patent protection is defined completely and totally in the claims of the patent. Any information in the patent application that does not support or relate to the claims is damaging.

When a patent attorney finishes a draft of a patent application, the inventor reviews it. The inventor almost never reviews the claims but usually reads the description thoroughly. At the end of this process, the inventor believes that there is protection for everything contained in the application.

Legally, the only protection comes from the claims, not the description. In fact, anything extra in the description hurts the company.

---

7   This is one example of why it is a good idea to keep continuation applications open on early patents. This book does not discuss this strategy in detail.

How is it damaging (other than the prior art problems described in the previous section)?

Information that is disclosed and not claimed are trade secrets that are being handing over to competitors free of charge.

Remember that the *quid pro quo* with the government is that the patent applicant discloses trade secrets in exchange for the patent. The purpose is so that competitors can use the patentee's trade secrets to improve on the invention.

The "kitchen sink" patent application—especially the ones done at the beginning of a company—often lay out the complete business and technology plans of a company. This can be gold to a competitor and give them deep insights into the startup's plans. Is this a good thing? No.

3.5.3 Where to Look for the Next Batch of Patents

The best patents have data to back them up. While every patent can have some prophetic elements, the best ones are based on real technology or market data.

As a company brings a product to market, the company solves various problems that make the product possible. The entrepreneur often sees these problems as a nuisance, but they are often the most valuable patents in the portfolio.

Valuable patents are those that solve the same problems competitors will have to solve.

Patents on the best way to solve a problem that competitors will face can protect a business much better than a patent on the end product. For example, a business may produce toothbrushes that have a pumice polisher. It may be just as effective—if not more so—to have a patent on a <u>mechanism to attach</u> the pumice polisher than to have a patent on the toothbrush with the pumice polisher.

These inventions pop up when it takes some effort from the engineering staff to solve a problem. One way to find these inventions is to ask the engineers what was the hardest problem they had to solve on this product?

These patents have the technical data of a problem solved to help justify the patent investment. In some fields, such as chemistry and biotechnologies, the examiners expect to see actual test data.

From a business standpoint, these patents can be easy to analyze from a design-around alternative. In the example above, nobody had ever figured out how to <u>attach</u> the pumice polisher to a toothbrush. A patent covering the attachment mechanism would likely be:

- easier to get through the patent office,
- broader than the prophetic patent on the toothbrush,
- much more effective at preventing competition; and,
- have outbound licensing potential.

A patent on attaching the pumice polisher could be used for putting pumice polishers not just on toothbrushes, but to other personal care products such as fingernail polishers, foot care products, and the like. The pumice polishers could be added to scrubbing and cleaning products like pot and dish scrubbers, toilet cleaning brushes, countertop cleaning brushes, floor scrubbers, and many others. There are probably many industrial uses as well, such as inside grinding and finishing machinery, and so forth.

This patent could be widely licensed into many different industries. One use might be to trade this patent in an exclusive cross license that would give the company the exclusive right to another company's technology within the personal health industry in exchange for that company's exclusive right to the pumice polisher in their industry.

These types of patents that come out of the problems solved in product development often are some of the most valuable technical advances and are often some of the most overlooked.

Valuable patents capture customer value.

Whenever possible, patent claims should focus on the customer's problem and solutions for it. These inventions come from the market data—not from the engineers.

Sometimes, identifying the problem is where the invention happens.

For example, an automated paper towel dispenser solves the problem of being exposed to germs after washing your hands.

The patent claims could be written to have motors, sensors, and all the components in a specific configuration—or the claims could be written about a device that produces a paper towel without a user's touch. In the first case, patents would have to be filed for every version of an automated towel dispenser and inevitably, someone could design around the claims. In the second case, a single set of claims could capture the entire market.

The first type of patent—the one with the motors and sensors—is something that would come from the engineers who are focused on the solution. The second type of patent—the one that described the customer problem (no touch towel dispensing)—comes from marketing. The second one is problem or market-focused, not technology-focused.

These types of patent claims come from market-related data. No-touch paper towel dispensing is a marketing message, not a technology message, because it focuses on a problem that consumers may or may not know that they had. Once the consumers are aware of the problem, all of the competitor's paper towel dispensers look like dirty, germ-infested petri dishes.

In many cases, the market-related inventions came after extensive trial and error. Market research and understanding consumer reactions are every bit as difficult—and valuable—as the research performed by engineers who build the products. When those insights come, they are excellent fodder for patent protection.

Sadly, the marketing and sales professionals are not as familiar with the patent process as the engineers, so getting a patent is not their go-to thing. Marketing and sales professionals are constantly talking to customers and are at a high risk of disclosing the invention to customers before the patent is filed, which is a big problem.

3.5.4 Building Out the Portfolio in Response to Business Signals

As the startup enters the market, there will be multiple course corrections. Problems with the technology will be corrected, but the market responses will also cause the product to morph and change.

Entrepreneurs have a vision of what the market wants, but often the market wants something different. A good entrepreneur will test several different go-to-market strategies, including different ways of reaching customers, different value propositions, different product configurations, and different pricing models.

A good entrepreneur will develop ways of identifying the signal from all the noise. What are the key elements that resonate with the consumers? The engineers thought that the pumice polishers in the toothbrushes were the defining feature, but the consumers may have liked the unique colors of the packaging.

An entrepreneur is wrong more times that right, but good entrepreneurs are constantly learning and responding to what the market says is important. With each data point that can be validated, there is learning, and with learning, there should be some consideration as to whether a patent would help (or harm) business exploitation of that learning.

Patents are not the only tool in the toolbox but can be a very efficient and economical way of making business moves in some circumstances; many of those circumstances are discussed in this book.

For example, a startup company may know that a bigger competitor is already in their space but does not understand the problem as well as the startup, and therefore the big competitor cannot develop as strong a solution as the startup. These insights can be patented, which makes the startup a much stronger acquisition target but also positions the startup to cross-license technology with the competitor if the big competitor were to assert their patents.

In another example, a company's products may be receiving a good market response and generating great cash flow. However, the market trends are towards miniaturization. One or two early prophetic patents might be useful to address the technical problems of miniaturization, followed by some data-driven patents as those problems are solved and have market validation.

A well-run company will add patents to their arsenal of tools for responding to business needs.

3.5.5 Culling the Herd

It is very hard to walk away from a pending patent application or even an issued patent.[8] In many ways, the patent application represents the hopes and dreams of the inventor and, by extension, the company. The patent is a business tool, however, and tough decisions have to be made when those tools are not providing value.

Culling the herd comes down to two basic forms—abandonment and sale. When is the right time to abandon a patent application? When should an issued patent be sold off? Both of these decisions should be relatively easy to make when the asset no longer aligns with the business objectives.

When should a patent application be abandoned?

Abandoning a patent application can happen for different reasons, but often it occurs when prior art pops up that severely changes the business value of the patent.

These decisions can be easy when there is a due diligence package done ahead of time. The due diligence package may include assumptions for the scope and breadth of the possible patent, along with the business value of the patent if it were to issue with the assumed scope.

When an examiner finds a prior art reference that severely changes the scope of the claims, the decision to go forward or not should come from re-running the analysis done during due diligence and making a decision.

The analysis will verify that the due diligence assumptions are still valid, and if not, the due diligence analysis should be updated.

---

8   Patent abandonment is the greatest fear of any patent attorney, so be prepared for a litany of reasons why a patent should not be abandoned.

Sometimes, the changes in the patent scope during prosecution may change the business case for the patent. Again, the due diligence analysis would be re-run.

It is easy to fall into the *sunk cost fallacy*. Sunk costs have no bearing on whether or not to proceed. Any cost analysis should be based on whether paying for the next step in prosecution is a good investment on a risk adjusted basis. Will the investment in the next step yield a useful asset with a meaningful risk-adjusted return?

As the examination process continues, the risks become more clear. When the examiner cites a very close prior art reference, the risk that a patent will never issue with our intended scope greatly increases. When the examiner has a hard time putting together an argument to reject our claims, the risk decreases.

When should a patent be sold off?

In the US, maintenance fees are paid at 3.5 years, 7.5 years, and 11.5 years after the patent issues. These are the classic decision points for asking whether or not to invest more money in a patent. If the maintenance fees are not paid, the patent will lapse and be dedicated to the public.

Startup companies typically are no longer a startup when they have enough patent assets to worry about paying maintenance fees, but larger companies with big portfolios incur giant costs at these intervals; many large companies try to sell off the patents or let them go abandoned at these points.

For a startup, a periodic review of their patent portfolio may identify patents that they are no longer using. When that occurs, a decision may be made to sell or license the asset.

Usually, the startup's patents come from the history of product development, and so most of the patents should remain relevant. However, when there is a significant pivot to the company's product and thinking, there may be some unused assets.

Patents that are not infringed will have *de minimus* value. There may be value to transfer the patent assets to a new company which may seek funding and try to learn from the first company's mistakes, but in general, liquidating a startup's uninfringed patents are often not worth the effort.

However, the due diligence package should identify possible infringers at the time the patent is written.[9] A list of possible buyers of the asset can be formed from the possible infringers, and a professional patent broker may be able to render a judgment as to whether they think the patents can be sold and for how much.

3.5.6 Selling on the Secondary Patent Market

The secondary patent market often appears to be a deep, dark mysterious place where huge deals get done. In truth, it is not all that mysterious and not that many huge deals get done.

The secondary patent market is where patents get traded. The players are the people liquidating assets, people acquiring assets, and the brokers and other people in between.

Several companies have been formed to try to establish a single market, but nobody has been able to generate enough momentum to consolidate the market. These include auction houses, patent listing services, and other systems.

Part of the mystery is that most acquirers do not want other people to know that they are acquiring. A big company that wants to move into a big market typically acquires patents in that market prior to making a move. Once word gets out that Big Co is buying patents, the prices rocket skyward and they can no longer get assets at a reasonable price. Further, as the word gets out, patent owners in the space start putting together war chests to enforce their patents to make it doubly difficult for Big Co.

The guide through this morass is a patent broker, and specifically, a seller's agent. These are people who sell portfolios for a living. They have a deep Rolodex of names and can get an audience when they have good assets to sell. They also have an ear to the ground and know who is buying and why they are buying. Brokers charge

---

9 It feels like an expensive and painful process to document this knowledge, but it is infinitely helpful when making business decisions about the patents over the patent's 20 year lifetime.

20-25% of the transaction price, and it may take six months to three years before they can sell an asset.

The secondary market is fueled by assets that are infringed. It is impolite to say "infringed;" the proper term is "evidence of use." Basically, the only patents traded on the secondary market are those where there is solid evidence that another company is using the invention. Patents without evidence of use are of no interest to brokers in this market.

Typically, a portfolio might have one or two killer patents that are infringed and a pile of other related patents that are not infringed. These usually sell as a bunch and credit is only given for the good patents. The rest are just fluff.

The secondary market is where a startup can unload assets that it is no longer using. Some companies try to keep a non-exclusive license for itself. This can be done, but it will devalue the assets and make them harder to sell.

Before selling patents, spend a lot of time looking for a good broker. It is somewhat like looking for a good used car salesman, but interview two or more brokers and ask them about their own reputation as well as the reputation of the other brokers being interviewed.

The ideal thing is to ask the broker's customers, which would be a patent buyer at a big company. It is a pretty small world, and these deals are based on relationships.

The secondary market is ever changing, with people entering and exiting quickly and new business models popping up repeatedly. A good broker will know about them and be a guide through the maze.

An important thing to note: the secondary market is where the good patents are separated from the bad ones. Only a small percentage of patents actually get traded, and those that do are well written, well prosecuted, and have solid commercial value. A broker only cares about top-drawer, investment-grade patents that have solid evidence of use.

3.6 Quirks of the Attorney/Client Relationship

The attorney/client relationship is not well understood by clients, and sadly, sometimes not well understood by attorneys. There is a lot of weirdness in the relationship, brought on by the conflict between fiduciary duties and the need for the attorney to run their own business.

3.6.1 Nuances and Artifacts of the Attorney/Client Relationship

The attorney client relationship is one of the fundamental tenants of our system of jurisprudence.

The attorney is an agent of the client and has a *fiduciary duty* to the client. This is because the attorney is often representing the client in their moment of greatest need. The agency relationship means that the attorney must do whatever the client wants. The *fiduciary duty* means that the attorney is responsible for doing the best job possible for the client.

The artifacts of this relationship come out in weird ways that are heightened in patent law.

Don't ask the barber if you need a haircut.

A favorite joke: How can a patent attorney tell a good invention from a bad one? It is whether the check clears.

This joke highlights the misalignment of interests, but there is far, far more history and nuance behind it. The point is not that the attorneys are bad people, but that our system of representation works in a specific way and has wrinkles that are not readily apparent to the clients.

There is such an enormous financial potential of a single patent that throws the normal attorney client relationship out of whack. A single patent might be worth hundreds of millions of dollars, and a single act by the patent attorney might ruin the entire thing. That is an enormous rock constantly hanging overhead, ready to fall.

3.6.2 The Attorney is an Agent of the Client

The agency relationship follows the "taxi rule": taxis are required to take the next person in the queue and to drive them wherever they want to go. The taxi cannot pick and choose their fare, and once the person is in the car, the driver must take them to wherever they want to go, even if they change their mind. With patents, the rule comes out like this:

Everybody deserves their day in court, and every crackpot inventor with a perpetual motion machine deserves their day at the Patent Office.

Attorneys will decline to represent an inventor for only a small handful of reasons, but the most common one is a conflict. Patent attorneys are exposed to a company's deepest, darkest (technology and business) secrets and cannot represent two companies that might compete, so they sometimes conflicted out of representing someone.

Clients often forget that they are merely one of many nameless, faceless inventors in the giant patent factory. For the clients, their patent represents their hopes and dreams and often a lifetime achievement personally and for their business. For the attorney, the patent is just one of hundreds and has no special value.

Of course, patent attorneys are trained to make the inventor feel special. The attorneys are taught to shake the inventor's hand and say congratulations whenever the patent application is filed or when a patent issues. The inventors almost salivate on command when the attorney praises the inventors with statements like "this is one of the best inventions I have seen."

All of these techniques are designed to build the inventor's undying loyalty but often mask the attorney's sloppy workmanship. The amazing thing is to see inventors who feel that they have a deep, intense, personal relationship with their attorney while the attorney barely knows who the inventor is. [10]

---

10 A best practice to select a patent attorney is to have another patent attorney review the first patent attorney's work product. Ask the reviewing attorney questions like "is this patent enforceable?", "where are the weaknesses in this patent?", "what would you do differently?", and similar questions. Selecting a patent attorney should be based on the quality of actual work product and not based on how nice they are.

3.6.3 The Fiduciary Duty of the Attorney

The fiduciary duty means the client can sue the attorney if the attorney does not act in the client's best interest at all times. The attorney carries malpractice insurance just for this occasion.

This is where a lot of weirdness comes out.

An attorney's fiduciary duty <u>prevents</u> giving meaningful business advice.

Inside the business of patent law, small inventors are known as "walking malpractice suits." Patent attorneys are taught to never give business advice. Instead, they merely explain all the options and make the client choose. Then the attorney is not on the hook.

Considering the liability of the attorney, this makes perfect sense. If an attorney tells a client **not** to get a patent, but five years later, that product is flying off the shelves, the attorney gets sued giving bad advice—and rightly so.

The attorney's liability in this case is almost unbounded. The attorney will be liable for all the profits the client would have made for the next 17 years in every country of the world. The liability could reach into the billions.

But consider the alternative: if the patent attorney says "get a patent" and they are wrong because the patent never issues, the attorney might be on the hook for $56,000, the approximate cost of a patent. Their malpractice insurance will cover this exposure, but mostly the attorney will point to the examiner or some other factor as to why the patent never issued.

But there are more problems.

3.6.4 Divided Interests

The patent attorney serves many masters. On one hand, the patent attorney is supposed to represent the business, but the patent attorney needs to keep the inventor happy. Besides, the attorney has a business to run and needs to keep the lights on.

There is often conflict between what the inventor wants and what is good for the company.

The patent attorney works hand in hand with the inventor but represents the client. In general, the CEO of a startup is happy with the patent attorney when their CTO/inventor is happy with the patent attorney. The inventor tends to be the gatekeeper between the attorney and the actual client.

The problem is that the inventors often demand certain things about the patent application that are not in the best interests of the client. Inventors are, by nature, a temperamental and fickle bunch, and they think they know best—about everything.

Many inventors see a patent as their personal reward that the company bestowed on them, but they do not understand that the patent is a business asset that will be used in many different ways over the next 20 years. [11]

Some inventors can get very prickly and demanding, especially when reviewing the patent application. This puts the patent attorney in a bind. The attorney needs to smooth over things with the inventor because the inventor is the gatekeeper to the attorney getting paid. However, the attorney is supposed to do the best thing for the company.

This results in pacifying the inventor at the expense of the ultimate client. Sometimes, the patent attorney will add whatever material the inventor wants, then just change it after filing.

The outside attorney has a business to run.

The attorney runs a business, and like all businesses, needs to make money. The attorney sells hours—either explicitly through the billable hour, or implicitly through fixed fee work—and the attorney needs to sell as many as possible. This is the source of most attorney jokes because it is true.

Clients are always frustrated because they cannot tell if they need to have the attorney do something because it is necessary or because the attorney just wants to get paid.

---

11   The patent term is 20 years from the date of filing or 17 years from the date of issue, whichever is longer—subject to a bunch of exceptions.

The classic example is a patent infringement opinion letter by an attorney. These letters investigate whether or not a company's product infringes someone else's patent. Many of these letters are an exercise in the attorney avoiding liability, with endless boilerplate about how no analysis is ever complete, that there may be changes in case law, that a judge or jury may view the patent differently, and on and on. The attorney spent most of their time avoiding liability and very little time on the substantive issue: is there evidence of infringement, yes or no?

3.6.5 Patent Attorneys Typically Have Little Business Experience

One little wrinkle of patent law is that patent attorneys and patent agents must have an engineering or science degree to sit for the patent bar exam. Very few engineers go to law school as most engineers make big money as regular engineers.

Consequently, there are very, very few patent attorneys compared to the general population of attorneys. The US has 1,200,000 attorneys, but only 31,000 are patent attorneys. Of the 31,000 patent attorneys, probably fewer than a quarter of them write patents.

The net result is that patent attorneys tend to be much more highly paid than regular attorneys, and they wind up doing the one thing that nobody else in the law firm can do: get patents through the USPTO.

The effect is that patent attorneys do not have direct experience in litigation, licensing, patent brokering, or any of the "business" side of things. Yes, there are patent attorneys who "help" with litigation, licensing, and the like, but they often are working under a conventional litigator or transactional attorney.

What does it mean for a client?

It means that if the patent attorney is an expert at writing good patents and getting them through the USPTO, that patent attorney is likely to not be very good at the business end. If they claim to be good at the business end, they are likely not to be expert at patent preparation.

The end result:

The company has the responsibility to make sure that the patents meet its business goals--not the patent attorney.

There are many things working against the company at this point. The patent attorney might know or have inklings that the company is headed down the wrong path, but the attorney's liability and their livelihood are at stake, so is the patent attorney going to speak up? Even if they do, they will only do so when they are absolutely, unmistakably certain that they are not missing something. Even then, the client is probably not getting the full story.

4 Due Diligence On Startups

Part of due diligence is the process of turning over the rocks to see if something is hiding. As investors, we want to know if problems exist as early as possible. The other part is to test the validity of assumptions to see if they are true. This gives us confidence to make the investment.

Sometimes problems exist when the entrepreneur hides things, sugar-coats things, or is just plain ignorant about the right way to do something.

For due diligence on patents, there are three major considerations: does the company actually have access to the patents, do the patents have any problem areas, and what are the patents worth. This section follows up with a few best practices that need to be in place before making an investment.

4.1 Assignments and Provenance

Assignments are the mechanism to transfer title of a patent, just like deeds are used to transfer real estate.

Assignments are recorded at the USPTO and are available to the public. On the USPTO website[1], a search for the company or inventor will show assignments as they are recorded. This website will show that an assignment exists and the parties to the assignment, but to get an actual copy of the assignment someone needs to visit the USPTO in person. There are third party services that will get the USPTO copies for a fee.

One of the flexible things about assignments is that different rights to a patent can be assigned to different people. For example, a patent can be assigned to a third party but can grant the previous owner a paid up, royalty-free license to use the technology. These provisions are only shown in the documents available at the USPTO and not online.

---

1   See http://assignment.uspto.gov.

For due diligence, the owners of the patents should provide all of the assignments in a chain of title. The chain of title always starts with the inventor and will progress to the current owner. If there are any license agreements relating to the patents, each of the previous owners of the patents should provide copies of the agreements.

Startups typically use assignments that come from their patent attorneys. Normally, these are ok, but often these assignments were written years ago and have been reused for decades since the patent attorney started practicing.

One of the items most often omitted is the right to "causes of action", which include the rights to sue for past damages. This is not important when the invention is created, because there is no past infringement, but it is important when patents are transferred later on.

Another thing to look for in the chain of title are any security interests in the assets. Just like a mechanic's lien on real estate, the patents may be put up as collateral for a bank or some other institution. This typically does not happen in startups, but these will appear from time to time.

In most cases, a quick look at the USPTO assignments database will show the provenance of the asset. The inventor, patent attorney, or company should have the signed assignments for review.

4.1.1 What if there are no Assignments?

For young startups or first time inventors, there may be no assignments at all. When this problem is encountered, <u>no investment should be made for three months</u>.

The USPTO assignment rules are a race/notice policy. An assignee has three months to file an assignment, otherwise an earlier filed assignment will have priority.

This means that there is a possibility that the patents were assigned to someone else in the last three months, and that person has not yet filed the assignment with the USPTO.

When there are no assignments recorded and the patent application has been around for a long time, the assignee must file an assignment, then wait three months to see if any other assignments are filed. If the three months pass without incident, the assignment is valid.

There are all sorts of scenarios where an entrepreneur, hungry for money, assigns their patents to someone for cash. They might not even know that it happened, as it could have been in a stack of papers or even a paragraph in some deal they signed.

The company needs to have solid chain of title to the assets. Until that is set in stone, stay away from the investment.

4.1.2 Inventorship Issues

Inventorship issues are one quick way to sink a patent. One of the worst things that someone can uncover is that there are problems with who was listed on the patent.

When patents get litigated, the patents can be attacked on the merits by arguing that the patent was issued incorrectly or that the patent examiner did not interpret the prior art correctly. This is long and tedious.

One of the easiest ways to kill the patent completely is to argue that the inventors were incorrectly listed. If there was any impropriety, the patent can be completely invalidated without ever arguing whether or not it was properly granted.[2]

These problems come in two forms: people who are listed as inventors but should not have been, and people who are left off.

4.1.3 Having Too Many Inventors

Courtesy in Asia is that an inventor will always list their boss on a patent. This can happen in startups, too, where the CEO might not have anything to do with the invention, even though their name was listed first. When looking at a patent portfolio, especially with

---

2   Note that this is a feature of US law. In the US, patents are granted to "inventors", but every other country, patents are granted to "applicants", which can be an inventor or a corporation. The recent patent law now allows the applicant to be a corporation, but only after the inventor assigned their rights to the corporation.

a long list of inventors, investigate who all the inventors are and what their area of expertise is.[3]

Here is a typical scenario where everything falls apart: Let's assume that the names of a six-person startup team are all listed as inventors on a patent. The CEO (or the patent attorney) is too cowardly to tell one of the people that they did not contribute, so the CEO magnanimously adds everybody to the patent. What actually happens is that the person who actually contributed the biggest portion of the ideas is quiet, but very resentful.

When the patent is being litigated, or when an acquiring company is doing due diligence before they buy the company, someone asks about all the people listed on the patent. By the time this happens, some of the people have left the company. The investigator calls all of the inventors, because they are listed on the face of the patent, and asks about how the invention took place.

Inevitably, the inventor who was scorned will go into a tirade about how so-and-so was included on the patent when they contributed nothing. Alternatively, the inventor may state that they had absolutely nothing to do with the invention but they were included for some reason.

All of a sudden, the patent can be completely invalidated with a simple affidavit from the scorned inventor. When that asset is a key to the entire acquisition deal, it can fall apart completely.

4.1.4 Having Not Enough Inventors

On the other side of the coin, what about leaving off an inventor?

These problems are less severe mostly because they are harder to uncover. We do not have a list of people on the face of the patent to call. However, there is one place where this happens quite frequently:

---

3   The legal definition is that a joint inventor or co-inventor must contribute at least one limitation to at least one claim to be listed as an inventor. The key here is that inventors must contribute to something that is in the final version of the claims. Often claims are amended and the inventorship is supposed to be updated, but this rarely happens in practice.

Patents with even the hint of inventorship issues are severely discounted in the secondary market and have almost no value.

Patents that come from startup accelerator companies have half the value.

Within the patent valuation community, the value of a patent of any company in a startup accelerator must be cut in two. Why is that?

The problem is inventorship, and here's the scenario:

A bunch of startups are put in a big room and put through their paces. They learn lean startup methods, they hone their pitch, they build a minimum viable product, they get some customer data, they hone their pitch some more, and they present to investors.

All of these companies work elbow-to-elbow with each other. A CTO from one startup might be standing by the water cooler struggling with their minimum viable product, and a CTO from a second company may be there, too. The first CTO explains the problem and the second CTO offers a suggestion. The light bulb goes off and they find the key that unlocks the product. The first CTO gets a patent on the invention, but the second CTO believes (rightly or wrongly) that they contributed to the invention.

The value of the patents for accelerator companies is cut in half because there is no way for the second CTO to be listed on the first CTO's patent. If they do list both inventors, both companies would have rights to the patent. If they do not list both inventors, the second CTO can cause the patent to be invalid.

The value is discounted 50% because there is a very strong possibility that another person in another company believes (rightly or wrongly) that they should have been an inventor but they were left off the patent.

It really does not matter if that person should have legally been listed as an inventor or not; what matters is what that person <u>believes</u>. The mere fact that someone is out there making noise that they should have been an inventor is enough to scare buyers away for good.

A simple transfer agreement at the beginning of the accelerator would have prevented all of these problems. A sample agreement is available at: http://www.blueironip.com/join-an-accelerator-and-lose-your-intellectual-property/.

4.1.5 Patents and Proprietary Information Agreements

Every person, including the original founder, must have a patents and proprietary information agreement in place with the company.

These agreements cause all of the inventions created by the person to be assigned to the company.[4]

Founders are notorious for not having these agreements in place. They will often have them with employees, but the solo founder often will not sign one with the company. As an investor, this must be in place with everyone—including the inventor/founder.

These agreements are essential because they cause the company to be the owner of the invention <u>at the time the document is signed</u>. Once the document is in place, it can be substituted as a regular assignment and sent to the USPTO as an assignment. This is incredibly helpful when there are problems down the road, such as when an inventor leaves the company or decides that they try to hold the patent hostage for some kind of bonus.

4.2 Good Patents are Easy to Read

If you can't understand a patent application, neither can the patent examiner, nor the infringer, nor anyone who will buy the company.

Sometimes, the technology is very complicated, and the patent application will reflect that. But when the document is virtually unintelligible, the value is severely discounted.

Unintelligible patents are the hallmark of patents written by someone who does not understand the invention or by someone who wants to make the patent so obtuse that they need to go to court. In either case, the patent does not have much value.

Many inventors boast that they did not understand their patent application because their attorney used "legalese." Some even joke that it was so dense that they did not even know if their invention was in there.

---

4   See *Stanford University v Roche Molecular Systems, Inc.* https://en.wikipedia.org/wiki/Stanford_University_v._Roche_Molecular_Systems,_Inc. The key point is that the agreement between the employee and employer must state that the employee "hereby assigns" their inventions, not "will assign" their inventions.

Make no mistake about it: a good patent is easy to read. It is difficult to write a clear description, and it takes ingenuity, thoughtfulness, and a big effort (read: motivation) to fully understand the invention, digest it to its essence, and write a clear description.

The key to good writing comes from sixth grade book reports: clear topic sentences for every paragraph, clear and simple sentence structure, and direct, active voice whenever possible.

Why does it hurt a patent when it is badly written? The first and foremost way it hurts is that the attorney did not understand the invention and probably made omissions or errors in describing the invention, not to mention the problems with examination and assertion that were covered elsewhere in this book.

Many people might say that they are not a technical or legal expert and incorrectly assume that they should not understand the patent. This is not true.

Patents are business documents that are read and understood by real people, not attorneys. When the patent is litigated, the patent is read by a judge and jury, who are common, ordinary people. If a normal person cannot understand the patent, neither can they.

For badly written patents, the risk factors include a higher possibility of Inter Partes Reexamination (IPR) reversal, difficulty of licensing or selling the patent, and general uncertainty about what the patent actually means. Discounting for all those risks, a badly written patent may have no value whatsoever.

4.3 References Cited

The best way to show that a patent has value is to have the examiner consider lots of prior art during the examination. In the US, we have the opportunity to send a list of patents, websites, scientific papers, and other documents for them to consider.

A patent with five references cited, all of which were found by the examiner, is a patent that is very weak and has a higher likelihood of being overturned by Inter Partes Reexamination.

A patent with twenty, forty, even 100 patents and prior art cited, is a patent that just "feels" strong.

Patents with lots of cited references are worth much more than those with few references.

One of the easiest ways for infringers to challenge an issued patent is through the Inter Partes Reexamination process, commonly known as IPR. To successfully challenge a patent, someone has to produce a prior art document that would have changed the examiner's mind.

The prior art can come from anywhere. A classic example is some master's degree thesis that sits on a dusty shelf of some foreign university.

The toolset used by examiners includes incredibly powerful search systems, but these are understandably focused on patent prior art and much less on scientific papers and websites, although these types of prior art are cited from time to time.

How to make a patent immune to Inter Partes Reexamination?

The best way is to get as much relevant prior art in front of the examiner and let them consider all of it. If a patent may be challenged by someone in the market based on their existing products, make sure the examiner has documentation about that product.

One of the reasons why people don't do this is because they are afraid that their patent would not be granted if the examiner looked at all the prior art.

A startup _wants_ the patent challenged as much as possible through the examination period. The more prior art considered by the examiner, the stronger that patent will be—and the less likely that it will be challenged by IPR.

When patent due diligence includes analyses of competing products and potential licensees, use that information to find documentation about competing products and send those to the examiner.

One quick way to assess patent quality is to look at the list of cited prior art for an issued patent. If there are only 4-5 references, all with little stars indicating that they were cited by the examiner, there is a good chance that a searcher could find something to challenge the patent for an IPR proceeding. If there are lots of references, especially non-patent references that show competitor's products, the patent is probably very strong.

Please note that there are ways to game the system. Some people cite lots and lots of useless and irrelevant references in their cases. Even if the references are irrelevant, the resulting patent is much more impressive with the references, and it will score higher in the automated scoring systems that some big companies use to assess patent value.

4.4 Invention Rating Checklist

An invention rating checklist is provided in Appendix A. A free downloadable PDF version of the checklist is available at http://investinginpatents.com/bonuses.[5]

The checklist has several areas of interest, each of which has a score to enter 1 through 5. Each value has a description that helps rate the invention.

These metrics represent hard-fought data that come from many different sources, and all reflect years of experience.

The checklist does not guarantee success—not by any means—but it does reflect a set of core metrics that should be used to evaluate inventions and patents. The purpose is to cull out inventions that would have little commercial value in order to invest in ones that do.

These metrics are designed to be used in the invention process, but they also have the same applicability to evaluating existing patents, or claims of a patent that is being examined.

How to use the checklist.

The checklist is an attempt to quantify several subjective measures. Each person may have biases or viewpoints that may adversely affect their scores.

---

5   This link also has other useful and downloadable content that supplements this book. The link is a free bonus for readers or purchasers of this book.

The best way to get a true sense of an invention's value is to have a group of people perform the valuation, then aggregate the scores. When a score is consistent between reviewers, the score is likely close to reality.[6]

When a score varies significantly between reviewers, there should be some discussion to figure out why. Often, one person may be seeing the invention in a much different way than the other, and a discussion will bring about a consensus to the most likely value.

Do not read too much into the total score.

The total score may be deceiving. Two inventions may have the same total score, but when an invention has a "1" for detectability and may be completely undetectable, that may kill the analysis.

There are some inventions that have such an enormous market potential that they would be good patents even with very poor detectability scores. But other inventions with higher detectability but low market potential would be poorer inventions.

The decision to invest in a patent is very much a business decision, and there are tradeoffs.

The checklist is one way to highlight the strengths and weaknesses of an invention so that those business decisions can be made.

Look hard at the inventions. This is business.

Inventors (and startup CEOs) are notorious for overselling their inventions. They have a deep love for their ideas and their businesses, and they can overlook even blatant problems.

This is business. Try to look at the invention with the completely dispassionate, unemotional view that the marketplace will have. The more realistic and honest the evaluation, the more accurate the assessment of the invention will be.

The real value of an invention or a patent comes from business execution.

The Checklist helps evaluating inventions or patents on the *speculative* value of the invention. The real value comes from actual

---

6   Of course, a consistent score could show an institutional or consistent bias.

execution of a business that brings the product to market. A high score only indicates that there is a better *probability* that an invention will be valuable compared to another invention. However, the real value comes from the hard work of the entrepreneur: successfully bringing a new product to market.[7]

4.4.1 Novelty and Non-Obviousness

Novelty and non-obviousness are the two factors used by the examiners to determine whether or not an invention should be patented.[8]

Novelty is relatively easy to understand: has anyone done this before? That answer is actually quite black and white.

But there is a scale of novelty.[9] Not every invention is as unique as the next. Some are routine solutions to a known problem, which may border on obvious. Other inventions are solutions taken from other industries and applied to the problem. Still other inventions use science that is new to the industry or technology.

G. S. Altshuller analyzed 200,000 patents and assigned a "level of inventiveness" to each one.

Level 1: obvious, routine solution.

Level 2: solution not well known in the industry, requires creative thinking.

Level 3: applies engineering knowledge from other industries or technologies.

Level 4: improvement uses science that is new to the industry or technology.

Level 5: new scientific phenomena are applied.

---

7 As will be seen in the next section, Thomas Edison's light bulb patent would probably only rate a 3 or 4 on the novelty scale.

8 In the parlance of PCT applications and European Patent Office, the terms are "novelty" and "inventive step". There are some subtle legal differences between non-obviousness and inventive step, but the concepts are largely interchangeable.

9 This scale of novelty is derived from TRIZICS by Gordon Cameron, 2010, pg. 7-10. Mr. Cameron derived his analysis from G.S. Altshuller, the Russian author of TRIZ, an incredibly powerful tool for inventing.

The results of Altshuller's study found that the patents were…

Level 1: inventiveness represents 32% of the patents, and can be thought of as taking less than 10 trials to create.

Level 2: inventiveness represents 45% of the patents, and take up to 100 trials.

Level 3: inventiveness represents 18% of the patents, and take up to 1000 trials.

Level 4: inventiveness represents a mere 4% of the patents, and take up to 10,000 trials.

Level 5: inventiveness represents less than 1% of the patents, and takes over 10,000,000 trials.

DISTRIBUTION OF PATENTS BASED ON NOVELTY

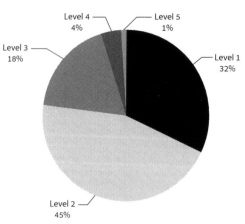

Figure 2 Distribution of Patents Based on Levels of Novelty

Something to note from the chart is that nearly half of the patents surveyed (45%) were level 2, and a vast majority (77%) were either level 1 or level 2.

When analyzing a large set of inventions, the inventions should have a similar distribution where less than 1% are level 5, and 77% are levels 1 or 2. Inventors consistently over value their inventions two or three levels higher than they really are.

As a comparison, Edison's light bulb patent would have had a level 3 for novelty. The lightbulb filament famously took Edison 1,000 tries to perfect, which corresponds with level 3.

This does not mean that the patent was not valuable, but it highlights the fact that the value of the patent comes from business execution.

Non-obviousness is difficult to quantify.

When the examiners perform their search, they try to find an exact match between the claims and prior art. Often, they will not find an exact match but they will find something close, and then combine that reference with another one which, when viewed side by side, will be "obvious."

For example, a claim might state that a product has a specific color, such as red. The examiner might be able to find the exact same product in another patent, but that patent might only say that the color is blue. The examiner would find another reference that says blue and red are functionally equivalent (or may just state it without justification) and reject the patent.

There are several arguments that are typically made to the examiner to show that the invention is non-obvious. The purpose of this book is not to go through an exhaustive list, but just to touch on this point:

The applicant must have a convincing story for the examiner to show unexpected results or some kind of "ah-ha" moment.

In the red product invention example, the argument could be that changing the color made it work better in certain situations that no one anticipated. Another argument may be that the industry was going in one direction and the inventor decided to go in the complete opposite direction.

Many inventions involve automating steps that are normally performed by hand (or could be performed by hand). In some cases, using a computer to do a repetitive task can have benefits that would never have been possible with paper and pencil.[10]

Let's assume that an invention automates a manual task, and that the manual task could be done ten times a day and result in 10 data

---

10   This discussion relates to the recent *Alice v CLS Bank* case from the US Supreme Court. *Alice Corp. Pty. Ltd. v. CLS Bank Intern.*, 134 S. Ct. 2347 (2014).

points. By automating the task, a computer can generate 100,000 data points in the same time.

On the face, this could be construed under *Alice* to merely automate a previously manual operation.

The unexpected benefits may be that large scale trends can be uncovered when analyzing 100,000 data points rather than merely 10. The further benefits are that large scale automation may allow for more accurate data checking and comparisons, meaning that improper results or anomalies can be detected. All of these benefits would not be possible with a pure manual version.

Patent searches and non-obviousness.

A patent search is the preferred way to find out if an invention is novel, but it is still difficult to figure out if it is non-obvious.

The results of a patent search will be the closest prior art. In many cases, the examiner will reject the case and say it was obvious in view of the closest prior art. To overcome the rejection, the applicant needs to have a solid argument about why the invention is not obvious.

It is very hard to guess how an examiner will view the invention and how they will make an obviousness argument.

However, when the closest prior art is very close, the obviousness argument may be impossible to overcome. If a patent attorney performs the search, they will always be pushing to file a patent, while knowing that the patent would be incredibly narrow.[11]

The only search that counts is the one the examiner does.

There is a point of diminishing returns on patent searches prior to filing. No matter how much searching is done before writing the patent application, the examiner's search is the one that counts.

Rather than spend a huge amount of money on searches, just send it to the examiner and see what they say.

---

11   Note that the patent examination process will be much more complex and drawn out when there are close prior art problems. This means a long and profitable prosecution process—for the attorney.

4.4.2 Detectability

Undetectable infringement makes a patent worthless.

Detectability is a measurement of how difficult it would be for someone to detect that an infringer actually infringes a patent.

Detectability is ranked based on difficulty. On the high end, some inventions are detectable based on casual inspection. Often, a competitor will advertise the feature as a compelling reason to buy their product.

Sometimes, detection might not be so obvious and would only be known after targeted investigation.

Sometimes, infringement is detected only by subject matter experts, and sometimes it may take insider knowledge about how something works.

Still other times, it may be utterly impossible to detect that someone infringes.

Level 1: Undetectable without specific knowledge about implementation.

Level 2: Detectable through experimentation by subject matter experts.

Level 3: Detectable through targeted investigation and experimentation.

Level 4: Detectable through inference based on observation.

Level 5: Detectable through casual inspection/competitor advertising.

Lots of products are impossible to detect.

Let's consider a software product. Many times, a software product executes deep in the bowels of a datacenter or inside a device. If there is no way to know that a competitor is running the same algorithm, the patent is completely undetectable.[12]

---

12   Software inventions are notoriously hard to detect, which is why the valuable ones tend to protect interfaces, such as user interfaces or Application Programming Interfaces (APIs). It should not be lost on the reader that detectability of software patents parallels the concept of capturing the observable commercial value of the invention.

Sometimes, hardware inventions are hard to detect. For example, an inventive clock circuit on an integrated circuit might only be detectable by reverse engineering the IC chip and removing each layer, then mapping the circuitry. This can be a painful and tedious process, but may be worth the effort for extremely high value inventions.

A chemical or manufacturing process may be completely undetectable when the process is performed inside a factory and there are no telltale signs of the process.

The more detectable, the better. When the invention is not detectable, it is almost always a good candidate to maintain as a trade secret.

Every word in the claim is important.

Remember to analyze the claims, not the description of the invention, when analyzing detectability. The claims are the strict legal definition of the invention.

Ask whether or not detection is possible for the <u>exact words</u> in the claim. In a method claim, could someone tell that a competitor did the <u>exact</u> method of the claim? In a product claim, could someone tell that a competitor's product was <u>exactly</u> like in the claim? [13]

For something to be detectable, a person should be able to verify each and every element of the claim. If there is one small item, no matter how small, that is required in the claim but cannot be detected, the patent does not have much value.

Inventors like to brush off detectability by saying that they can infer that infringement has occurred. The inference is often based on the inventor's belief that their way of doing the invention is the "best" and nobody would possibly do it any other way. [14]

This argument does not hold water.

---

13   When considering an invention prior to patenting, building a set of claims first is essential to performing this analysis.

14   This is an artifact of a myopic inventor who has been concentrating on their invention for so long that it is the only "right" way of solving the problem. Their solution is often well optimized for their specific problem, but there are many other business cases where the "non-optimized" solution might have value.

Infringement requires solid, provable evidence that holds up in court. If there is any way possible that someone could do the invention, <u>even if it was not perfectly optimized like our invention</u>, the patent is not enforceable.

Overcoming detectability issues.

One way to overcome a detectability problem is to look for artifacts or telltale signs of the invention.

For lots of software inventions, a good practice is to focus on the interfaces of the software product, rather than the guts of the product. A patent on a sophisticated algorithm that automatically underwrites mortgages, for example, may be completely undetectable.

However, an application programming interface that accepted a borrower's credit card history and returned a yes or no decision on a mortgage would be perfectly detectable and enforceable. After making that change to the focus of the invention, we might do another patent search to determine whether or not we could get a patent on the application programming interface.

4.4.3 Actor Analysis

Another very important factor to consider is the actor in the invention. There are some actors that can be sued, and others that cannot. Further, when two or more actors are in a claim, there is a problem of divided infringement.

The actor analysis has several different levels, from bad to good:

Level 1: Two or more actors, all of which are customers or a single actor who is immune from litigation.

Level 2: Two actors, one is a deep pocketed competitor.

Level 3: One actor who is a customer, but has deep pockets.

Level 4: One actor who does not compete, but has deep pockets.

Level 5: One actor who is a direct competitor and has deep pockets.

This analysis is not linear, meaning these levels are not evenly divided steps. They are arranged in order of preference.

Some business cases support a patent directed at a customer that has deep pockets when other factors are present. For example, a product sold to enterprise customers may be protected by claiming actions that the customer would perform. This situation may be somewhat acceptable because it might keep the customer from building the product in-house.

It would be preferred to have the patent directed at a competitor, but sometimes that is not possible given the specific invention.

Direct infringement by a consumer or customer makes a patent worthless.

An example is helpful.

Consider an invention of heat-moldable insert for a shoe, such as a ski boot. The invention was originally conceived as heating up the insert in boiling water, forming it to the user's foot, and inserting it in the ski boot.

Who is the infringer?

It is the customer. Can the customer be sued? No. Does the patent have any value? No.[15]

A patent that claims a method of use, like our example above, may not be enforceable when trying to stop copycat importers from overseas. These kinds of claims are not very likely to be enforceable by the International Trade Council, which is the best way to hold up shipments of infringing goods.

There are many different ways to express claims.

In the example above, the claims are "method-of-use" claims. These tend to be one of the weakest types of claims but some of the easiest to get. In many cases, method of use claims can capture the business value of the invention succinctly and broadly.

---

15   There are other ways to enforce the patent, such as the legal theories of inducement, contributory infringement, and others, but those enforcement mechanisms are much weaker than direct infringement.

Another way to claim an invention is a product claim. Product claims are some of the strongest claims because they are easy to detect and they capture the product that would be produced by a competitor.[16]

In some cases, product and process claims can get intermingled, where the product claims require certain operations or installation conditions to be met. These claims can cause lots of actor problems as well.

How to overcome actor problems.

In the example, the claims can be rewritten to focus on the product produced by a competing manufacturer. In the example, the claims could be rewritten as a plastic component that gets soft at one temperature and hard at another temperature and has a specific shape.

The rewritten claims now focus on a specific actor that we are targeting. The business case for the patent is to stop competitors from manufacturing a competing product.

Software products often are difficult to patent because two or more actors combine. Sometimes it is very hard to write a patent claim where the consumer or end user performs an action, then the computer does something in response.

A best practice is to stand in the place of the device and write a method claim that "receives input from a user."

Another aspect of a software product is that various pieces are often performed by different parties. As software platforms evolve, there are services that specialize in the most mundane aspects of a solution, such as software-as-a-service providers for authentication, payment processing, or whatever.

Be mindful of the fact that software platforms and services are ever changing, and focus the invention on a relatively narrow value added element or point of novelty. As a product goes to market, some aspects may be 'outsourced' to other providers who have an API specifically designed to do some aspect of the product.

---

16   There are several other ways to claim an invention. This is not a comprehensive list, but merely a couple of examples to help illustrate the thought process of evaluating claims.

The best way to use actor analysis is to reform an invention to focus on the point of novelty that the products or services provide. Ideally, the point of novelty is also the customer benefit.

Protecting the razor/razor blade product.

Two actor claims are those that require two different people to perform the invention. One actor may be a supplier of a non-reusable part (e.g. a razor blade) while another may be a supplier of the reusable part (e.g., the razor). These types of patents are notoriously hard to enforce, and therefore tend to be worthless.

A better way to focus the claims in the razor example would be to focus on the *mechanism that attaches* the razor blades to the razor. Two patents (or at least two sets of claims) would be written: one describing only the mechanism on the razor side, and a second describing only the mechanism on the razor blade side. In this way, the two patents could be used to license razor blade manufacturers to provide compatible blades, or to license razor manufacturers when the company wishes to provide the blades.

4.4.4 Design Around Analysis

The baseline for all economic valuation of an invention is the best alternative to the invention. The easiest way to find the best alternative is to attempt to design around the invention.

Once the invention is identified, the inventor (or sometimes a separate set of inventors) will try to "design around" the invention.

This should be viewed from the technology standpoint, by looking at different technical solutions to the same problem.

It should also be viewed from the business standpoint, by trying to envision different ways a customer might solve the problem—or ways that they might live with the problem.

There is ALWAYS an alternative to the design.

How many times does a CEO/inventor tell people "there is nothing like it"? This is just not true—or if it is, it proves that nobody wants the product.

In some cases, the best design around alternative is actually better than the invention. By going through this analysis, it may better hone the business value of the invention. With some inventions, the invention may have advantages in one set of circumstances and disadvantages in others.

Once the best alternative is identified, the economic advantages of the invention should be determined. The economic advantage calculation should be as detailed as time may allow. In many circumstances, a back-of-the-envelope calculation may be sufficient to bracket the value of the invention.

The design around analysis considers two factors.

A comparison of the invention to the best design around alternative:

Level 1: Best alternative is superior in cost/performance to invention.

Level 2: Best alternative is equivalent to invention in cost or performance.

Level 3: Best alternative is missing important features of invention.

Level 4: Invention has 5x performance advantage over best alternative.

Level 5: Invention has 10x performance advantage over best alternative.

A comparison of the true economic advantage of the invention:

Level 1: Invention no economic advantage.

Level 2: Invention has economic advantage of 1.5x.

Level 3: Invention has economic advantage of 2x.

Level 4: Invention has economic advantage of 4x.

Level 5: Invention has economic advantage of 10x or greater.

In these analyses, we are trying to establish the value of the *contribution* of the invention to an overall product.

4.4.5 Alignment With Internal Business Goals

Patents protect a business only when the patents are directly related to the products being produced. This analysis considers two factors: how close the product is to shipping; and how key the invention is to the product's value.

The invention can be graded using a first set of metrics:

Level 1: No resources assigned to invention.

Level 2: Feasibility stage only.

Level 3: Resources are devoted to implementation.

Level 4: The invention is likely to ship in the next product release.

Level 5: The invention is shipped or committed to ship.

The second aspect is how important the invention is to the products.

Level 1: Supplemental aspect of product.

Level 2: Improvement to product.

Level 3: Key feature of product.

Level 4: Important aspect of product strategy.

Level 5: Key aspect of product strategy and product roadmap.

The goal of this analysis is to ensure that the patents focus on inventions that are important to the products are going into the marketplace.

4.4.6 Alignment to External Business Possibilities

External business possibilities add value to a patent because they open the door to licensing the invention to other companies. The single best way to get acquired is by having products and patents that fit into a competitor's portfolio.

This analysis considers three parts of the problem: how well does the invention fit with a competitor's products and strategy; the outbound licensing potential of the invention as a standalone product; and the likelihood that competitors will adapt the invention as a standard.

For the product fit in the competitor's portfolio, we consider:

Level 1: No known or expected competitor activity.

Level 2: Solid improvement to competitor's product where different solutions exist.

Level 3: Address a shortcoming in a competitor's product that a third party may implement.

Level 4: Addresses a shortcoming of competitor's product in a substantial manner.

Level 5: Addresses direct need of competitor's product and fits in competitor's strategy.

For the outbound licensing analysis:

Level 1: No expected licensing potential—invention limited to our products/technology.

Level 2: Invention could be licensed as part of a package with other inventions.

Level 3: Invention as good value in other markets.

Level 4: Invention has very significant value in other markets (i.e., dramatic cost savings or improvements).

Level 5: Invention has significant value and is a key element of a licensable product for other markets.

For the standards-related analysis:

Level 1: Not expected to be used by competitors.

Level 2: Market has no preference for invention over competing options.

Level 3: Some competitors may adopt.

Level 4: Most competitors are likely to adopt.

Level 5: Likely to become standard in all competing products.

4.5 Patent Searching

A patent search is a starting point for any analysis of patents. They are done under different circumstances and for different reasons, but they all can be done with the same basic techniques.[17]

A search is helpful when investigating a technology, when considering getting a patent on an idea, when determining who are the big players in a market, or when considering an investment.

Searching uses a classification system called the Cooperative Patent Classification (CPC) system. All patents are classified using this system, and it acts as the Dewey Decimal System in a library, where all patents describing the same technology are grouped together.

The CPC is the most universal of the different patent classification systems, and the USPTO has recently changed from its older USPC system to CPC. CPC is also used by the European Patent Office, and the CPC has become the gold standard for patent searches.

Some searchers are very familiar with the classification system and begin by searching the classification system to find the best classes, then search patents within the class.

When a searcher is not familiar with the classification system, a keyword or natural language search can uncover several patents. From the patents that appear to be close to the invention, find the appropriate classes, then search within those classes.

The classifications of a patent or patent application are listed on the front page of the document or in the search results. Here is an example from a search for "birthday balloon" from Google's patent search engine:

---

17   The purpose of this section is to just give a general feel for how a patent search is done and is not a comprehensive tutorial.

Musical balloon

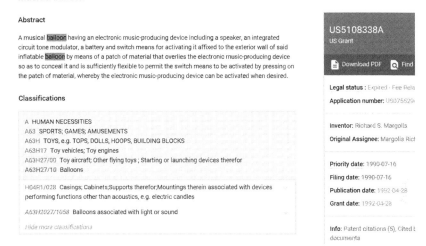

Abstract

A musical balloon having an electronic music-producing device including a speaker, an integrated circuit tone modulator, a battery and switch means for activating it affixed to the exterior wall of said inflatable balloon by means of a patch of material that overlies the electronic music-producing device so as to conceal it and is sufficiently flexible to permit the switch means to be activated by pressing on the patch of material, whereby the electronic music-producing device can be activated when desired.

Classifications

A HUMAN NECESSITIES
A63 SPORTS; GAMES; AMUSEMENTS
A63H TOYS, e.g. TOPS, DOLLS, HOOPS, BUILDING BLOCKS
A63H17 Toy vehicles; Toy engines
A63H27/00 Toy aircraft; Other flying toys ; Starting or launching devices therefor
A63H27/10 Balloons

H04R1/028 Casings; Cabinets;Supports therefor;Mountings therein associated with devices performing functions other than acoustics, e.g. electric candles

A63H2027/1058 Balloons associated with light or sound

Hide more classifications

US5108338A
US Grant

📄 Download PDF   🔍 Find

Legal status : Expired - Fee Rela
Application number: US075529

Inventor: Richard S. Margolis
Original Assignee: Margolis Rich

Priority date: 1990-07-16
Filing date: 1990-07-16
Publication date: 1992-04-28
Grant date: 1992-04-28

Info: Patent citations (5), Cited t documents

Figure 3 Partial Search Result from Google for Birthday Balloon.

Under the "classifications" section (shown expanded) are the classes that this patent was given. The top classification of A63H27/10 is expanded to show the hierarchy of classes. By clicking on one of the class numbers, a list of all the patents within that class can be searched. By adding keywords to search within the specific class, a reasonable search can be done in minutes.

Some classifications are very well organized, while others are not. Remember that there is an influx of hundreds of thousands of new patents and patent applications added every year, so the classification system is continually growing, with new subclasses being added and other classes being reorganized.

Many paid-for search engines, such as AcclaimIP.com, will have powerful tools for navigating the patent system as well as finding additional data that comes from aggregating several databases.

One of the powerful features of AcclaimIP is a list of all the patent owners in a classification and the patents that were purchased in that classification over time.

The list of patent owners often uncovers companies that would not have been considered a competitor. By listing the number of patents owned by each competitor in the specific class, a researcher can easily see who might be a formidable competitor.

Diving into a specific competitor's portfolio in a specific class will reveal their technical and business approach to the same problem as our invention.

An example of a search results for a "zip-lock" plastic bag is shown below:

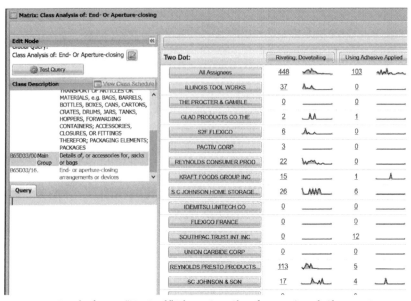

Figure 4 Results from a "Zip-Lock" Plastic Bag Classification Search Showing Patent Owners and Recent Acquisitions. Data from AcclaimIP.com. Used with permission.

This view shows the number of patents purchased by a company and sparklines that illustrate the priority data of those patents. From this view, we can see that Reynolds, S.C. Johnson, and Illinois Tool Works are active acquirers. These companies would be targets for any new inventions in this field.

4.6 How to do Valuation Analysis

Valuation analysis of patents can be very involved, and every analysis has very big assumptions.

The value of a patent to a startup cannot always be quantified in dollars. For example, the deterrence factor of keeping competitors at bay because the company has a patent can never be quantified or even estimated.

Patents have values based on use scenarios. The patent may have one valuation in an outbound licensing scenario but a different value if the patent were sold outright.

The most common valuation method revolves around a reasonable expected royalty. This method is used most often by the courts to assess penalties for infringement.

The easiest method is the 25% rule.[18] This rule of thumb is that a reasonable royalty rate for a patent would be 25% of the gross margins of a product protected by the patent. These is still debate on whether it is 25% of the entire gross margins of the product or 25% of the contribution of the invention to the gross margins of the product.

For example, a reasonable royalty rate for an intermittent windshield wiper patent might be 25% of the gross margins of the windshield wiper, but sometimes the courts have awarded 25% of the gross margins of the entire car. One could argue either way, and there would be endless lawsuits to decide this.

There are many more sophisticated methods for determining valuation, but each one has one or two assumptions on which the valuation hinges. Most of the work is to uncover data that supports those assumptions, or to try and bracket the assumptions to give a reasonable range.

One key element of valuation: remember to consider the patent life. A patent with 15 years of life can have a very significant value when evaluating the licensing revenues on a discounted cash flow basis.

After all the analysis, the patent is worth what someone is willing to pay. The valuation procedures are a way to find good order-of-magnitude numbers for valuation.

---

18   The 25% Rule is discussed in "Use Of The 25 Per Cent Rule In Valuing IP" by Robert Goldscheider, et al., available at: http://www.bu.edu/otd/files/2009/11/goldscheider-25-percent-rule.pdf.

5   Conclusion

We at BlueIron use all the tools and techniques in this book when we evaluate inventions and move them through the patent process.

We are investors. Our mindset is that the patent must have economic value to be worth the investment, and we cannot waste our time and money chasing vanity patents. We certainly cannot waste our time doing the job poorly, as that hurts us incredibly.

We do due diligence like our livelihood depends on it—because it does.

Logic tells us that some of the inventions we finance will not be as good as others, and statistics tell us that we need to beat the average. We believe that by using these metrics for screening inventions and these techniques for due diligence beforehand, we will have a much better chance at beating the average.

It is our hope that you can use the techniques in this book to better your investments. Hopefully, you can spot problem areas in a portfolio company and help guide a CEO to make better decisions, as well as spot possible investments where things are being done well and double down.

Appendix A
Invention Ratings Checklist

Invention Rating Checklist, Part 1
PATENT WORTHINESS

Here we determine if we could get a patent and if it would be enforceable. If the invention is not detectable, try reforming the invention so that it could be. Likewise, adjust the focus of the invention to read on the right actor. Remember that you cannot enforce your patent against your customer, only your competitor.

NOVELTY

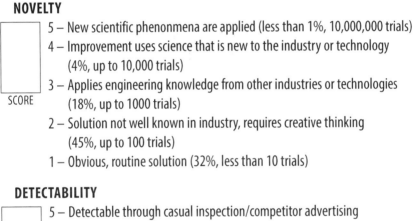

SCORE

5 – New scientific phenonmena are applied (less than 1%, 10,000,000 trials)
4 – Improvement uses science that is new to the industry or technology (4%, up to 10,000 trials)
3 – Applies engineering knowledge from other industries or technologies (18%, up to 1000 trials)
2 – Solution not well known in industry, requires creative thinking (45%, up to 100 trials)
1 – Obvious, routine solution (32%, less than 10 trials)

DETECTABILITY

SCORE

5 – Detectable through casual inspection/competitor advertising
4 – Detectable through inference based on observation
3 – Detectable through targeted investigation and experimentation
2 – Detectable through experimentation by subject matter experts
1 – Undetectable without specific knowledge about implementation

ACTOR ANALYSIS

SCORE

5 – One actor who is a direct competitor and has deep pockets
4 – One actor who does not compete, but has deep pockets
3 – One actor who is a customer, but had deep pockets
2 – Two actors, one is a deep pocketed competitor
1 – Two or more actors, all of which are customers or a single actor who is immune to litigation

Invention Rating Checklist, Part 2

DESIGN AROUND ANALYSIS

Compare the invention against the best alternative design. The best alternative can be a product in the market, or how you might design a product to compete with the invention. There ALWAYS is an alternative to your design.

COMPARISON OF INVENTION TO BEST DESIGN AROUND ALTERNATIVE

5 – Invention has 10x performance advantage over best alternative
4 – Invention has 4x performance advantage over best alternative
3 – Best design around alternative is missing important features of invention
2 – Best design around alternative is equivalent to invention in cost/performance
SCORE 1 – Best design around alternative is superior in cost/performance to invention

TRUE ECONOMIC ADVANTAGE OF INVENTION

5 – Invention has economic advantage over alternative of 10x or greater
4 – Invention has economic advantage over alternative of 4x
3 – Invention has economic advantage over alternative of 2x
2 – Invention has economic advantage over alternative of 1.5x
SCORE 1 – Invention has no economic advantage over alternative

Invention Rating Checklist, Part 3

INTERNAL BUSINESS VALUE

We want to know how well the invention fits in our existing product line.

ALIGNMENT TO INTERNAL BUSINESS PLAN

5 – The invention is committed to ship
4 – The invention is likely to ship in the next product cycle
3 – Resources devoted to implementation
2 – Feasability stage only
SCORE 1 – No resources assigned to invention

IMPORTANCE TO PRODUCT

5 – Key aspect of product strategy and product roadmap
4 – Important aspect of product strategy
3 – Key feature of product
2 – Improvement to a product
SCORE 1 – Supplemental aspect of product

Invention Rating Checklist, Part 4

EXTERNAL BUSINESS VALUE

This section examines how well the invention fits into competitor's product lines, as well as the outbound licening potential and applicability to industry standards. This is where patents have a multiplying effect to make your company truly valuable.

COMPETITOR'S PRODUCT FIT

SCORE

5 – Addresses direct need of competitor's product and fits in competitor's strategy

4 – Addresses a shortcoming of competitor's product in a substantial manner

3 – Addresses a shortcoming of competitor's product that a third party may implement

2 – Solid improvment to competitor's product where different solutions exist

1 – No known or expected competitor activity

OUTBOUND LICENSING POTENTIAL

SCORE

5 – Invention has significant value and is a key element of a licensable product

4 – Invention has value in other markets (i.e., dramatic cost savings or improvement)

3 – Invention has good value in other markets

2 – Invention could be licensed as part of a package with other inventions

1 – No expected licensing potential—invention limited to our products/technology

APPLICABILITY TO INDUSTRY STANDARDS

SCORE

5 – Likely to become standard in all competing products

4 – Most competitors are likely to adopt

3 – Some competitors may adopt

2 – Market has no preference for invention over competing options

1 – Not expected to be used by competitors

Appendix B
What Good Patents Cost

The patent cost of $56,525 comes from a cost model based on the industry average for patents. These data are based on the American Intellectual Property Law Association (AIPLA) semi-annual report on fees charged by intellectual property lawyers for various functions.[1]

The average patent in the US costs $56,525.00 over its lifetime.

The semi-annual AIPLA report is the best standard for judging reasonable fees for IP work, including patent and trademark preparation and prosecution, litigation, and other IP-specific work. This report is used by lawyers nationwide as the benchmark for fees and includes breakdowns of fees from different locales, number of attorneys in a firm, practitioner experience, and other breakdowns of data.

This analysis uses the national average of all respondents as the baseline for setting fees. This cost model assumes small entity status and the 50% discount that the USPTO gives to small entities.

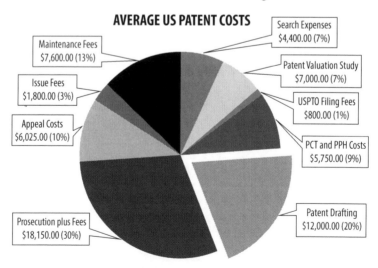

AVERAGE US PATENT COSTS

Search Expenses $4,400.00 (7%)

Patent Valuation Study $7,000.00 (7%)

USPTO Filing Fees $800.00 (1%)

PCT and PPH Costs $5,750.00 (9%)

Patent Drafting $12,000.00 (20%)

Maintenance Fees $7,600.00 (13%)

Issue Fees $1,800.00 (3%)

Appeal Costs $6,025.00 (10%)

Prosecution plus Fees $18,150.00 (30%)

---

1   See http://aipla.org. The most recent report came out in 2015. The figures in this section were derived from that report.

The cost of a patent has one large unknown: the cost of the examination. Some patents will be allowed at the first look by the examiner while others will languish as there are endless office actions and responses. It is not unusual for a patent to be pending for 5 or even 10 years.

The average patent application has 4.2 office actions. This value reflects the experience of several experienced attorneys as well as data from a very large company's 30,000+ patent portfolio. From this number, the number of Request for Continued Examinations (RCEs) are anticipated to be 1.5.

The likelihood of filing a pre-appeal brief is determined to be 0.75 per case. This value is again derived from analysis of approximately 300 recent cases prosecuted by surveyed practitioners. Of those cases for which a pre-appeal brief is filed, approximately 1/3rd are appealed to the full board and the remainder are either allowed or prosecution is reopened.

The fees used in the cost model are current as of the date of publication, and are based on small entity rates where applicable. Some of the fees, most notably PCT fees, can vary widely based on the case, and for this analysis, an approximate mean value is used.

Patent Preparation

Patent drafting costs are the initial investment made at the beginning of the patenting process. These include patent valuation analysis and patent searches, as well as drafting and filing the patent application in both the US and PCT. The total investment made at the time of filings is estimated at $26,950.00.[2]

---

2   Note that these costs include a substantial patent search ($4000) as well as a PCT application ($4650) that typical patent attorneys do not include in a quote. Without these two items, the average cost for filing a patent application would be $18,300. The PCT application is not required, but is useful for entering the Patent Prosecution Highway.

Patent Preparation	Expenditures		Attorney Costs	
Drafting	$	-	$	12,000.00
Search fees	$	400.00	$	4,000.00
Filing fees	$	800.00	$	-
PCT	$	3,500.00	$	1,250.00
PPH filing	$	-	$	1,000.00
Total:	$	4,700.00	$	18,250.00
Grand total:			$	22,950.00

Patent Prosecution

Patent prosecution costs are the costs associated with getting the patents through the US Patent and Trademark Office (USPTO). The average is 4.2 Office actions.

Appeals can be expensive but are anticipated to occur with only a fraction of the cases. The anticipated rate of a pre-appeal conference is three pre-appeal conferences in every four patent cases. In some stubborn cases, pre-appeal conferences occur two or three times for a single patent application, but the overall ratio is expected to hold true. This value is based on analysis of several hundred patent applications prosecuted by interviewed practitioners.

Similarly, a full appeal occurs in about 25% of the cases.

The estimated costs of pre-appeals and full appeals are averaged into the total estimated prosecution costs, and it should be noted that appeal-related costs can cause a single patent application to become very expensive.

Patent Prosecution US Office Actions	Expenditures		Attorney Costs	
Number	4.2		4.2	
Drafting	$	–	$	4,000.00
Total Office Actions	$	–	$	16,800.00
RCEs	1.5		1.5	
Prep/Filing	$	–	$	500.00
RCE Fee	$	400.00	$	–
Total RCE	$	600.00	$	750.00

Appeals

Appeal Fee	$	400.00	$	–
Pre Appeal Likelihood	0.75		0.75	
Pre Appeal Brief	$	–	$	4,000.00
Appeal Likelihood	0.25		0.25	
Appeal Brief	$	–	$	10,000.00
Total Appeal Cost attributable to Average Cost Model	$	400.00	$	5,625.00

US Issue

Issue Fee	$	800.00	$	–
Prep time	$	–	$	1,000.00
Total Issue Fee	$	800.00	$	1,000.00

Maintenance Fees

3.5 Year	$	800.00	$	100.00
7.5 Year	$	1,800.00	$	100.00
11.5 Year	$	3,500.00	$	100.00
Total Maintenance Fee	$	6,100.00	$	300.00

Totals	Expenditures		Attorney Costs	
Preparation	$	4,700.00	$	18,250.00
Prosecution[3]	$	1,800.00	$	23,175.00
Issue	$	800.00	$	1,000.00
Maintenance	$	6,100.00	$	1,500.00
Summary	$	12,600.00	$	43,925.00
	Grand Total:		$	56,525.00

---

3 Prosecution includes Office action responses, RCEs, and Appeals related costs.

Appendix C
The BlueIron Investment Model

A New Alternative Financing Mechanism for Startups: BlueIron IP

BlueIron IP is an investment company that finances patents for startups. BlueIron's non-dilutive financing for startups pays all of the patent costs, including filing fees and attorney's fees, using a conventional commercial "lease-back" arrangement.

This model has been gaining traction since its first release in the fall of 2014. After financing professional poker player Phil Gordon's patent for his new software startup, Chatbox, BlueIron has made investments in startup companies in software, hardware, biotechnology, medical devices, financial services, and agriculture.

"We have been gaining a lot of confidence with both startup CEOs and angel and venture capital investors," says Russ Krajec, CEO of BlueIron. "They see a tremendous amount of value not only in the financing, but in the due diligence prior to making an investment. We get called in on many angel deals just for our evaluation of the invention quality."

BlueIron IP is solves many problems by financing patents.

It is out of reach for a startup company to get high caliber, well researched, and well written patents. These patent applications require an enormous investment in time, money, and expertise— mostly by the patent professionals who curate the inventions, write the patents, and nurture them through the examination process.

Most startups resort to some terrible strategies, such as filing provisional applications and other cost-avoiding strategies that virtually guarantee poor results.

By financing the patents, BlueIron removes the cost barriers to getting good patents. This opens up the options to do a full due diligence workup, and when the invention is able to be financed, to file expedited applications.

BlueIron needs its portfolio companies to be successful.

BlueIron's investment in a patent only works when the client is successful, and vice versa. If the company is not successful, BlueIron's investment only generates a bunch of patents for products that never made it to the market, and those patent assets have very little value. If the company is successful, the patents have real value—far more value than the cost of the financing.

With BlueIron's financing, the startup does not have to worry about patent costs.

Since BlueIron provides all the financing, the patents can be expedited. BlueIron recommends using the PCT-Patent Prosecution Highway when available, which often results in an issued patent within 12 months. With PCT-PPH, the costs of the patent are compressed into a 12 month window, rather than spreading them out over 3-5 years. However, an issued patent is far more valuable to a startup company—especially one raising angel or venture capital—than a lowly pending application that may or may not ever issue.

With BlueIron's due diligence, the startup gets a much better patent asset.

Startup companies do not have the advantage that big companies do—professional, in-house patent counsel with sophisticated strategies for creating and managing their patent portfolios. BlueIron fills that void.

BlueIron does much more than an extensive patent search. BlueIron performs a thorough competitive analysis, analyzing the startup's competitors and looking at who is buying and selling patent assets in the space. The due diligence analysis knocks out a very large percentage of companies for financing, and BlueIron typically finances only 10% of the inventions it reviews.

While the financing justifies the relationship on the numbers alone, the fact that BlueIron puts in the due diligence beforehand and only writes patents that have direct business value, makes the BlueIron relationship incredibly powerful.

BlueIron invests in patents.

BlueIron approaches patents with an unabashedly detached and unemotional view. This is an investment, and it is treated as such. BlueIron's risk profile depends on avoiding the bad investments and cultivating the good ones in the same manner as an angel or venture capital investor.

BlueIron only invests in investment-grade ideas.

How does BlueIron evaluate inventions? BlueIron has an extensive due diligence process that it applies to each invention. Part of the process is an invention checklist, which is available at http://bit.ly/IPWChecklist.

How the investment model works.

BlueIron creates a new framework where both parties have the same goal: protect and grow the business.

BlueIron combines a conventional patent holding company/ licensing structure with a commercial "lease-back" financing model. The startup receives an exclusive license to the assets, which is transferrable to acquirers and always includes a buyout provision.

BlueIron's sole focus is to build investment-grade patents that have commercial value. By treating patents as "collateral," BlueIron's business model rises or falls based on how strong the patents are—and how successful the startup is.

The BlueIron financing structure puts BlueIron in the business of doing what it does best: building investment-grade patent portfolios. At the same time, the startup has more capital to deploy in the business.

BlueIron's thorough due diligence prior to financing has won the respect of angel investors, who value the tough stance on avoiding useless patents, as well as the guidance given to each startup for curating meaningful patent portfolios.

Investors appreciate the candid and thoughtful due diligence for their investment deals as well as the comfort that BlueIron is doing everything possible to build solid, investment-grade patent assets for their portfolio companies. As an added bonus, their portfolio companies are able to stretch their cash further because they are not paying patent attorneys.

BlueIron only invests in patents for operating companies, not for individual inventors for whom the invention is just a hobby. BlueIron invests in pre-revenue companies and at a very early stage, but must be a business with a financial commitment to bring a product to market.

Index

ABOUT THE AUTHOR

Russ Krajec is a patent attorney and CEO of BlueIron IP, an investment vehicle that finances patents for startups. Mr. Krajec holds a BS and MS in Mechanical Engineering from Rensselaer Polytechnic Institute and a JD from University of Denver (both fine hockey schools). Mr. Krajec co-founded Concurix Corporation, an angel and venture-backed startup company in the software space. Prior to law school, Mr. Krajec was an engineer with companies such as McDonnell Douglas, Maxtor, Hewlett Packard, and WaterPik. Mr. Krajec is an inventor on over 30 patents, and has authored close to 1000 patent applications for clients around the world.

51872705R00080

Made in the USA
Columbia, SC
25 February 2019